A BOOK OF LIGHT

A BOOK OF LIGHT

When a Loved One
Has a Different Mind

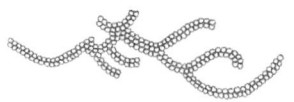

Edited by
JERRY PINTO

SPEAKING TIGER PUBLISHING PVT. LTD
4381/4 Ansari Road, Daryaganj,
New Delhi–110002, India

This anthology copyright © Speaking Tiger
Introduction copyright © Jerry Pinto

The copyright for individual essays and stories
vests in the respective authors

First published in India in hardback by Speaking Tiger 2016

ISBN: 978-93-86050-20-5
eISBN: 978-93-86050-18-2

10 9 8 7 6 5 4 3 2 1

Typeset in Adobe Garamond Pro by SÜRYA, New Delhi
Printed at Thomson Press (I) Ltd.

All rights reserved.
No part of this publication may be reproduced,
transmitted, or stored in a retrieval system, in any form or
by any means, electronic, mechanical, photocopying,
recording or otherwise, without the prior
permission of the publisher.

This book is sold subject to the condition that it shall not,
by way of trade or otherwise, be lent, resold, hired out,
or otherwise circulated, without the publisher's
prior consent, in any form of binding or cover
other than that in which it is published.

CONTENTS

Introduction   7

Papa, Elsewhere   15
   Sukant Deepak

My Mother the Professor   26
   Leela Chakravorty

My Mother's Breast   36
   Amandeep Sandhu

Mothers and Daughters   55
   Nirupama Dutt

Daniella   68
   Patricia Mukhim

The Man Under the Staircase   89
   Sharmila Joshi

Abhimanyu, Our Son   97
   Madhusudan Srinivas

Roger, Over and Out   101
   Lalita Iyer

CONTENTS

In My Mother's Shadow *Annabelle Furtado*	128
Dris *Manoj Menon*	138
Anna *Shashi Baliga*	144
'You Didn't Know Her When She Was Normal' *Parvana Boga Noorani*	155
Some Questions for a Brother *Ina Puri*	165
Notes on the Contributors	171

INTRODUCTION

My mother was bipolar. It began when I was born. For the next thirty-six years, she would make several attempts to kill herself. Of this material, I crafted a novel, *Em and the Big Hoom*, published by Ravi Singh in 2012. At one of the first readings that followed, a journalist whom I had thought of as a friend stood up and asked, 'Don't you feel guilty that you used your mother and her life to craft this beautiful book?'

Somehow I got through the moment and the rest of the evening without tears or rage, and I thought the toughest part was behind me.

But of course I was being optimistic.

Over the next few months, the readings I did went well enough, but the question-and-answer sessions that followed left me wondering what I had unleashed. 'I don't know what happens,' I said to a colleague, 'but these readings seem to become encounter groups. The last one had this woman who began to talk about how her family had locked her brother in his room for five years because he claimed that God was talking to him. It was only much later that they realized what was going on and got him psychiatric help.'

My colleague smiled and I had the uncomfortable feeling that she thought I was boasting.

INTRODUCTION

'I often don't know how to handle it,' I added. 'I'm not equipped to.'

'Perhaps all you have to do is listen,' she said.

A few days later, she wrote me a mail in which she suggested that I gather such stories and edit them, and create 'a book of light'—her words—which would illuminate these areas of darkness in the Indian middle-class family.

That evening, Parvana Boga Noorani called me and told me that she had tracked down my number through some friends because she had read *Em...* and it had reminded her of her journey with her own mother. We had so much in common, we discovered. The same hurts and vulnerabilities, the same fears, the same psychiatric wards, the same scramble to secure the new pills, the same desperate wish, sometimes, to be rid of it all. I asked Parvana if she would write and I took it as a good omen that she agreed, and so the first piece for *A Book of Light* began to take shape.

Over the next couple of years, I emailed many people who I knew had lived with similar afflictions of a loved one. I knew it was difficult ground; sometimes I was cutting close to the bone. Often, I had found out about the 'problem' when, in despair, I had been consulted about it. This would happen even before *Em...* was published, because I had always tried to be as open as possible about the fact that my mother had bipolar disorder. I had made a commitment to myself and to her and to our bond that it should be no more than saying 'My mother has diabetes', because it was all a matter of the wrong chemicals, an imbalance in the blood, a misfiring of neurons. If this sounds too much like some version of biological determinism, too easy a formulation, I can only say that we must all build our own defences against what causes us grief, and this was mine.

INTRODUCTION

Some people I spoke to told me memorable stories. An uncle, a doctor, who was bipolar but who had moved to Australia and into a small community where he was much loved and the entire town worked with him so that he could continue to practice. A grandmother who was lovely and wild and told bizarre stories that have haunted the creative impulses of her grand-daughters. A family with a brother and a sister who were both afflicted and both needed hospitalization… But these stories you will not find in the collection. One of them was short-circuited by the youngest generation of the family who did not want their grandfather's mental illness made public. The second was abandoned because the woman who wanted to tell it found that no one in the family would cooperate, so she was left with only the wisps of her own memories of her grandmother. The third story began well, but then the person writing it stopped responding to emails.

I realized this was *their* defence against what memory can bring back, what grief can do, and I tried to be respectful of their decision.

Others refused outright. I don't blame them, either. We have to shape our own stories and we do this as much by what we say as by what we do not say. And as author of the story of my life, it is only I who can decide what I am comfortable with and what I am not.

And so even in the editing of these stories, I have walked with care. Some of these people are my friends. They have held me riveted with their accounts of being chased by siblings with axes, of running blindly through fields to stop a mother from jumping into a well. Sometimes the pieces they wrote would lack some of these details. I would think: 'You told me of the time your father went after your sister with a meat cleaver. Do you want to put that in?' But I would ask only where I thought the relationship could bear

INTRODUCTION

the strain of my reminding them of what I had been told—often people are shocked at what they have revealed; or perhaps even more shocked that it has been remembered.

I have great respect for those who have told their stories here. They carry their torches bravely, shedding light on the dark areas of pain and guilt and utter helplessness. For it was in the family that these dramas of the mind were played out. In fiction and in cinema, we read of how people retreat into the family when they are hurt. There they are surrounded by love and warmth and they can lick their wounds in peace. But what if it is your mother who is wounding you and then soothing you by turns? What if it is your father who seems distant or desolate, living in a dark tower that you cannot enter? What if the *Sturm und Drang* is in the home? Where then is your refuge?

In some senses, of course, the 'normal home' is a myth. As the locus of all the most intense dramas of our lives, how can it ever be normal? Here are people who know us best; they know without being told what they must shield us from, and they know, when they wish to hurt us, where the chinks in our armour are. We all know that if we look hard enough, we'll see that the family is a human institution and therefore flawed. We have all thought 'What could I do without you?' as often as we have thought 'What am I going to do about you?'

But what of the family where all attention must suddenly be focused on one person who is suffering? What of the family where someone commits suicide and leaves behind a vacuum, a space that seems to mock every attempt at love and holding on? What of the family which must institutionalize one of its members? How does it manage?

INTRODUCTION

And after it's all done, how do you go back and talk about it? Why would you?

I cannot answer for the 'why'. I was often asked about catharsis after *Em*... 'Is it better now? Do you feel that you have let go of the past and moved on?' I didn't know how to answer this. I still don't. It would be easy enough to come up with something; only, that might hold out false hope. And if I did try to answer, what would it be? I might want to say 'Yes' on Monday and 'No' on Tuesday, and on Wednesday, 'Maybe, but only if we can agree on what catharsis means.' On Thursday I might say, 'Are you nuts?'; on Friday it could be, 'The function of a work of art is not to heal the artist but to heal the world'; and on Saturday, 'Yes, sometimes, though I would have to say not in general, but I don't even know about that for sure.' And on Sunday I might take a break and refuse to answer questions even to myself.

The only thing I can offer as some kind of answer is an image. You are on a long hike and your haversack is cutting into your shoulders. You ease your thumbs under the straps, peel the straps away and move them to another spot. For a moment, there is a huge feeling of relief, a rush of physical wellbeing at having eased the load. But soon the pressure begins somewhere else and the weight begins to bear down again. That doesn't mean it's something you live with every moment of your life. You can often set down your bag and dance; and then it's as if you soar. The burden will be back on your shoulder again, but for now, you soar.

But one thing I think I can go out on a limb and say: it doesn't get any easier or more bearable from *not* talking about it.

As for the 'how', you will see that two writers in the anthology have used narrative devices. They have told their stories using the

INTRODUCTION

tools of fiction, taking on the position of omniscient observer in one case and speaking from the afflicted mind in another. 'Aren't these distancing devices?' you might ask. But all writing demands some distancing devices. Some appear on the surface. Some lurk in the tonalities of the work: irony, for instance, or black humour. If you do not withdraw some distance, you can never tell the story. To each his or her own distance, to each his or her own device.

THE STORIES IN this book do not seek to hold out answers. They tell you what happened and how it was dealt with. You may often disagree with what was done or how it was done. This is inevitable. When my mother was ill, our family and friends were always full of advice. Some of it was helpful—cuttings from magazines about new remedies; names of doctors. Some of it was not—the name of a new 'healer' who asked you to inhale a powder that made you sneeze a terrible black fluid; suggestions not to take 'any of this' seriously, 'because these people are just malingering and if you don't give them any food, you'll see how quickly hunger makes them come round.' All of it was tiring because we were just about getting through the day and we didn't really need the critics on the sidelines telling us what a bad job we were doing.

We knew that already.

When your mother has tried to kill herself yet again, you know something is wrong. You know that things are falling apart and the blood-dimmed tide is loosed. You know that you could not hold back the demons, but you also know that whatever you tried was nothing compared to how much she herself struggled before she gave in. You know all this and sometimes it would just

INTRODUCTION

help if someone could come and be there, sit quietly and offer companionship, let you talk when you wanted to but let you be silent if that was what might help you heal.

Thank God there were friends like that, people like that. Driven more by instinct and empathy, they would say—or not say—the right thing. There were others who would simply stay away. That often hurt but it was, in the long run, a wise thing to do. No one needs the awkwardness generated by awkwardness, by the visitor who is driven by duty but wants to be a million miles away. No one has the psychic energy to face the vulgar curiosity of those who think mental illness is a spectator sport and want to ask 'How did she manage?' and 'Where were you guys?' and 'My, who cleaned up afterwards? What a mess it must have been!' That's bad enough, but it's even worse when you find yourself putting on an air of normalcy and answering questions with a pretended matter-of-factness. 'Oh, it just takes a minute or two of inattention,' you say, as if you were discussing the possibility of a soufflé collapsing. 'We were sleeping,' you say, trying not to feel guilty for doing something human. 'We cleared it up ourselves,' you say, suggesting calm capability. You hate yourself for doing this but at this time it is nice to talk normally to normal people. Later, other savage answers will come but nothing as savage as the accusations you turn on yourself.

There are no moral lessons in this book, or easy stories in which everything comes out right in the end. There will be questions you will want to ask: How did you deal with the molestation? Where do you think your father is now? Did you ever forgive your mother? Did she marry someone else? Your questions should reassure you of the veracity of these narratives. This is how life is. Open-ended. Challenging. Terrifying. Demanding of us all that we have, and then some.

INTRODUCTION

If you have a story that you would like to share, write to me at assignments.for.jerry@gmail.com. If you have a story that you would not like to share but still would like to commit to the word, write it down, record it, draw it, paint it, shape it in some way. I cannot assure you that it will help but it will not harm you.

Best wishes, then, because one of the decisions we have to make, on our own, is to turn towards the light.

February 2016   Jerry Pinto
                                                                                          Mumbai

PS: The title of this book was easy. The subtitle took some work. It's not about being politically correct; that position has been stigmatized so much and subjected to so many ill-advised and unaesthetic formulations, that its original intention—to protect people from verbal violence—has been forgotten. I wanted only to say: it's not easy to live with someone who has a psychiatric problem. I didn't know how to say it, and after asking all those who wrote for the book, I came up with this one.

And yes, this is a book about middle-class people whose biographies and destinies have allowed them to be able to write in English. In the vast majority of cases, it is to the exorcist or the priest that the family turns. Their stories are not represented here. I wish there were a way for this book to include them without othering them, exoticizing them into a colourful spectacle for our consumption. I could not find a way, nor could I find someone to write it.

PAPA, ELSEWHERE

Sukant Deepak

BETWEEN 3 AND 3.30 A.M. he would knock on the door of my room which was held in place delicately by a latch. He would call out my name. No, he would whisper it. For some time I would pretend that I couldn't hear anything. The knocking would then become persistent. I would get out of bed and go close to the door, but not open it. He would plead, 'Hit me on the head with a rod. I know you keep one under your bed. I know you can do it.' Each time, I would tell him to get lost. I would treat him like the dog we never had.

Then on the morning of 7th June 2006, he went for a walk and never returned. When we—my mother, my sister and I—were convinced that he was not coming back, there was a collective sigh of relief. There was almost a celebration.

'I hope we never see his face again,' my sister said. I hoped so too. So did my mother who taught chemistry for a living but loved the arts (well, she could reproduce Husain well).

SWADESH DEEPAK'S BIPOLAR disorder was diagnosed in the 1990s. By this time he had become a disgusting and despised figure for everyone: family, friends and relatives. Lying in the queen-sized bed in his room, this famed writer who would receive the Sangeet Natak Akademi award in 2004, would stare for hours on end at the ceiling. I would peep in, pretend not to be scared and retreat to my room. There was no question of praying. After all, posters of Marx and Lenin ruled the walls of my room in those days, sharing space with Cindy Crawford in a bikini.

The first suicide attempt happened in the year 1999. There was a lot of noise in the bathroom. Mother and sister rushed there. I was awake but did not move. It was night, after all; I should be asleep, I was not supposed to know. My cousin, a doctor, was called. She came with her husband, also a doctor. Both were sleepy but they managed to do what they were supposed to do. They thwarted his bid to take his life. The whole thing lasted around two hours. I did not move. Not an inch.

My cousin decided that it was time to take him to a psychiatrist now. He was taken to the Post-Graduate Institute of Medical Education and Research (PGI, for short) in Chandigarh, about an hour's drive from Ambala, where we lived (where I still live, in the same house). They gave him pills. He took them and slept for hours through the day. A few days later, he stopped taking the pills. It was time to suffer again. And not just for him.

In 1991 he had written the widely acclaimed Hindi play *Court Martial*. It was during the play's first show in Calcutta that he met a woman whom he called 'Mayavani'. He never forgot her. I remember asking him once the English translation of the word. He looked straight into my eyes and said, 'Do you really think English is rich enough to accommodate the power of Mayavani?' This from a man who taught MA English classes in a college in Ambala for twenty-six years. (I had to be content with my own loose and inadequate translation of Mayavani: The seductress of illusion.)

I also remember asking him why he was ill. What was actually wrong with him? Why didn't he take the medicines when doctors said that the disease could be treated? He said, 'That's a good question, for a change. Do you think black magic can be treated? More importantly, should it be treated, that too with some darn pills? I am ill because I insulted her, because I refused to reciprocate her love.'

'So I should never refuse to love a woman?'

'That can only happen if women show any interest in you. I mean your features are so beautiful, almost perfect, like your mother's. You don't have my rawness, my foul mouth, my imperfection, my charm. Only those women who are completely incapable of black magic will fall for you. You're lucky that way. But on a serious note, give your love to every woman who asks for it.'

He laughed after that. I laughed too. I loved his cruelty. My mother and sister hated it.

He had stopped going to the college by this time, insisting that he was too exhausted. In the initial years, it seemed more like depression than bipolar disorder. The man known for his fiery temper and fine ability to hurt us would take insults without retaliating now. Mother would make it a point to tell him exactly how things were the moment she came back from her school job: 'So, enjoying yourself while your wife runs the house? What a shameless man!' He would go quiet. If, that is, he had been saying anything at all. His walk became slower and he retreated to his room, a dark space filled with the heavy smoke from his unfiltered cigarettes.

I would, of course, join my mother. His presence was poison to me. How could someone who seemed absolutely healthy physically pretend that something was seriously wrong with him? I was in college now, the same college where he had taught. I never wanted to join it. What if the teachers asked me about him? Moreover, it was so desi. Most of my friends had moved to bigger cities. I didn't speak to many people in the college, not even the teachers. Most of them seemed like the students in my class—uneducated. Except the one man who didn't teach me.

One day, I went for a long walk to buy cigarettes. When I got back home a neighbour told me to go to Monga Hospital. Swadesh had tried to burn himself. I was composed. I just told myself, 'Another mess.'

I got on to my Enfield, took the longer route and rode right up to the gate of the hospital. Not because of any urgency, I cannot remember feeling any. I guess I just wanted to scare the people sitting there.

Mother was sitting with him. So were my doctor cousins. He was conscious. I asked him directly, 'What happened?'

'I would prefer not to answer such a stupid question. You can do better.'

The woman doctor there laughed. Then blushed, almost.

I could have killed him for that.

He was shifted back home after a few days.

A YEAR LATER he reminded me of the incident. He asked if I hadn't liked his answer mainly because the woman doctor, a burns specialist invited from some other hospital, was very attractive.

I said yes.

He loved my answer.

I had my revenge sometime later. Ours is a huge, ill-maintained, colonial-era bungalow, the kind one sees in horror films. We usually have several extra cooking-gas cylinders stored in a small room. (Even now, when I live alone, they are there.) He went to that store-room one day. When he didn't come out for a long time, my mother entered, just like an ill-trained spy in a bad Hindi film—walking with soft, deliberate steps. I heard her scream. This time, I moved fast. He was trying to set ablaze a cylinder with an old matchbox which he couldn't even hold properly as his right hand was still in a sling.

'You can do better,' I said.

He looked at me, wounded.

I took the matchbox from him and went to telephone the doctor cousins. In all the years with him, my mother had learnt the choicest of abuses in Hindi. She was using them quite effectively now while handling the man who was suddenly full of energy.

The doctors arrived in no time. My cousin's husband, as always, was very composed. He took Swadesh to his study and asked him to write a suicide note. He told him not to put a date.

My father smiled and whispered, 'Thanks. But you will make it happen, na?'

The doctor didn't reply and asked him to just write. The moment he started dictating the note, Swadesh interrupted, 'Spare me. You really think I need dictation, that too from you?'

I regret missing the look on the doctor's face.

Mother called up my sister, who was working with *The Indian Express* by now, and told her everything. My sister listened without comment. Senior people in PGI were contacted. There were no beds in the psychiatry ward. Perhaps my sister turned to her colleagues for help. A top editor called the director of PGI to get a bed in the burns ward and arrange for a consultation with psychiatrists who would see Swadesh in that ward. It was done so clinically and practically that it seemed...abnormal.

I preferred not to visit him much in the hospital. Mother went after school, practically living there. A senior police official, close to the family, had arranged for a guard to be present in the ward every day till the time she reached Chandigarh.

He stayed in the burns ward for four months. The scars from his old wounds hadn't yet healed completely, so he received treatment for these as well, this time not from an attractive woman doctor but the famed Dr Chari. Rumour had it that he was the doctor who had reconstructed Rajiv Gandhi's face after he was blown up by a suicide bomber. (By the way, Swadesh was the happiest when India had its Vietnam in Sri Lanka.)

Swadesh's sister, whom we were not very close to (we were not close to anyone from his side of the family except the doctor cousins), would be with my mother in the hospital, praying silently. She belonged to a generation that believed in prayers. Swadesh believed that his sister had a healing touch. He would wait for her to place her hand on his forehead. When she did, he would smile.

A special meeting was held in the psychiatric ward to discuss Swadesh's interesting case. It was not every day that one got to treat a major Hindi writer who preferred to communicate in English and believed that someone had him under a spell. Everyone wanted his case, or at least be a part of the team that dealt with his exorcism.

Ultimately, a short, very slim, bespectacled man, Dr Pratap

Sharan, was assigned the case. 'Please get all his short stories, novels and plays tomorrow,' he told my mother. After a pause he explained, 'I need to know what I am dealing with here.' When my mother said that she could tell him what the books were all about, he said, 'I am an educated man.' He paused. 'I can read. Please get them.' Then he walked away without waiting for her reaction.

A week after he got the books, Dr Sharan decided to meet Swadesh.

'Everybody is against me. No one presents my case. No one believes that Mayavani did this but that she should not be punished,' Swadesh told him.

The doctor spoke in short sentences. He loved his pauses. 'My name is Dr Pratap Sharan. I am your defence lawyer. I believe you completely when you say that Mayavani is responsible for all this. I also understand that she should not be punished.'

Swadesh was stunned. He liked the doctor instantly.

My mother bore quietly the torture of travelling forty kilometres to Chandigarh from Ambala every day. She did not explode. Not even once. She gave Swadesh a shower every day, and walked to the chemist shop which was in a different building to get his medicines.

But one day he said that his tooth hurt and she couldn't hold back. 'Look what you have reduced me to, you bastard. I was such a beautiful woman once; I look like a beggar now. Why don't you die?'

A young doctor attending to a patient stopped his work. Then he decided to walk out of the ward. Suddenly there was complete silence. An old woman from a village, someone's attendant, approached my mother, sat with her, caressed her arm lovingly. They were quiet together.

THE DOCTORS TRIED everything, including electro-convulsive (or 'shock') therapy. After four months we were asked to take him home, lest he thought that the hospital was the world.

'It would be dangerous to keep him here any longer,' Dr Sharan said, in the most un-dangerous way.

Swadesh was brought home in October. He looked at the garden for a long time. Autumn leaves from the peepal tree had engulfed the whole lawn. 'The grass must be feeling suffocated; you should have got it cleaned,' he said. 'The house seems smaller. And who stole our garden where I planted the roses?'

Nobody was in the mood to tell him that most of his plants had died as the gardener had gone to his native village in Uttar Pradesh. And we had better things to do than tend the huge garden which anyway was such a waste of space. Someone must have said that, because I remember him saying in what was no louder than a whisper: 'But the roses could have been watered. It wouldn't have taken much time.'

Swadesh's condition began improving within a month. He began his morning walks again. He started going to his favourite tea stall where daily wagers and labourers gathered in the evening. He was never the odd one out; most of the regulars knew him well. He would often carry an extra pack of cigarettes to give them. Perhaps the communist in him was most alive during his tea meetings.

At home, there were even times when he seemed to be aware of our existence. I had become a borderline alcoholic by then. Of course, everybody was worried. Swadesh tried to tell me several times that it made sense to start late in the evening and not during the day. I paid little attention, and for the next three years I lived in a hell of my own.

His quirky sense of humour was back. I stopped my motorcycle one evening when I saw him walking in the market and offered to drop him back. After about ten minutes, he asked me to stop.

'I didn't spend 55,000 rupees for you to ride a vehicle that moves at the speed of a rickshaw. I'd rather walk and reach faster.'

But what was most reassuring was that he had started writing his last work, the unique *Maine Mandu Nahin Dekha* (I Have Not Seen Mandu), chronicling his years as a psychiatric patient. I was the first to listen to his completed chapters. The solitary hero omnipresent in all his stories was now replaced by a man struggling to come to terms with the demons in his mind. There was no venom, just an eerie silence towards the world. He would spend hours in his study, working on the book at a pace we'd never seen before. Maybe he knew that he was going down again. As the days passed, we noticed that he had started eating less, and the walks, too, had become infrequent.

A close family member settled in the US offered to take him there for treatment. And he meant it. But Swadesh looked straight at him and said: 'I'd rather die than set foot in that bastard country.' Truth be told, he hated air travel because he was not allowed to smoke. Nicotine chewing gums were a strict no-no. 'I'd rather suffer than eat chewing gum. No graceful man should be seen like that,' he once told an air-hostess.

The memoir was completed and published in record time. A painting by his favourite painter, the late Jehangir Sabavala, was reproduced on the jacket. He should have been a happy man. But we noticed his complete lack of enthusiasm when he was opening the package containing the first copies of his last book.

We knew he was back to square one. We all were.

I shifted to Chandigarh to work for the *Hindustan Times*, leaving Mother alone to deal with him, his illness and her own bitterness. She encouraged me to go, insisting that it was important for me to breathe free. And I did. Wine, women and writing on art. I was having a wonderful time.

I used to go home on weekends. He would look forward to my visits, though he never said so. Except once: 'It's only on Saturdays that I'm constantly looking outside the door of my room. I like to see the motorcycle parked in the verandah.'

We would talk about books, what I was reading, the kind of features I was writing, the women I was seeing. 'I'm glad all your girlfriends are much older than you. I'm sure you get a lot of motherly affection after some experienced lovemaking.'

My mother hated these 'vulgar' conversations.

Years later, she told me that my Chandigarh landlord had called Swadesh and complained that too many women visited my barsati, and that he couldn't take it any longer. My father had told him politely, 'Well, you should tell him yourself. I don't interfere in people's personal lives,' and hung up.

IN JUNE 2006, Mother called. 'Swadesh has not come back since he went out yesterday.' I instantly knew that he was never coming back. I got the motorcycle refuelled, stopped at my favourite bar for two beers, and set off for Ambala. We decided to wait another day. He did not return. There was no note. His wristwatch, wallet and two torches, which he always kept by his side, were in his room.

We went to the cops the next day. I flashed my press ID and procedures were 'expedited'. They even offered me tea and a samosa.

PAPA, ELSEWHERE

The inspector told me that he had also got some calls from his seniors—my sister using her 'influence' again—and assured me that we would be informed by the evening.

'Informed about what?' I asked.

The cop looked at me and just kept looking at me for a while. Then he walked away.

It has been several years, but I haven't forgotten the police officer's face. Slim and borderline handsome.

Maybe after listening to Swadesh's history, he knew that people like him are never found.

No, we did not launch any massive search operation. We did not go to Haridwar, as suggested by some relatives. Yes, I did meet his psychiatrist once. 'Just pray that he is not alive,' he said. 'You have no idea what he must be going through without his Lithium.'

I know that he will never come back.

However, just to be sure, I still keep an iron rod under my bed.

MY MOTHER THE PROFESSOR

Leela Chakravorty

When, as a child, I returned home from school I would scream, 'Maaa...I'm home!' right at the gate. And there she would be, her thin cotton sari billowing, red and white bangles clinking as she waved. I'd run to her and she'd catch me in her warm embrace. This, I would think, as I burrowed into her arms, inhaling her fragrance, is my home. This is where I want to be.

My mother constituted my world. She taught me my first letters, she taught me poetry. She read me the poems of Sukumar Ray; she read me my first stories from Tagore. She introduced me to Shakespeare and to Mahasweta Devi.

I loved her as every child loves her mother; I loved her as no other child has ever loved her mother. Because that's what the bond between mother and child always is: it is universal and it is unique.

My mother made our love unique.

'Do you know how much pain I went through to bring you into this world?' my mother asked me once. No, not once, but again and again.

'Oh my God, you bitch, you swine, you whore, don't you love your mother?' she asked me, again and again.

'That guy is so handsome,' she would say, pointing to a man on the street, a random man. 'I want him to be my future son-in-law. Look how he's staring at you, I think he loves you.'

As her only child, her daughter, I knew I meant the world to my mother, Professor Reema Chakravorty. I just couldn't be sure what that world was like. I was, depending on her mood, a daughter, a friend, a bitch, a whore and in her last days, her nurse, her nanny, her doctor.

I was born on a chilly winter morning in a small town in the foothills around the Kanchenjunga peak. My mother told me that she did not experience any labour pains. Sometimes she told me I caused her unbearable pain. She returned to her mother's house when her pregnancy was advanced, as was the custom, but she said no one knew that I was due. I don't know how this was possible since she also told me that her sister had said, 'I will kick your bulging belly and kill your child,' when she got tired of fetching and carrying for her. But I got used to contradictions. And I got used to not contradicting her.

For this was not the only story I heard about my birth.

'The doctor asked, "Whom would you like to save: the mother or the baby?" Everyone sang out in unison, "The mother." Not your father though. Your father wasn't there. He was running away from me. Even then. Running away and giving tuitions while you were being born.'

I didn't know whether this was true. I didn't know if it was false.

At another time, she said: 'I lay on the operating table with my legs wide apart, even the anaesthesia was of no use to me.'

But you didn't have labour pains, Ma, I said in my head. *Why would you need anaesthesia?* But I knew better than to ask.

'I would not go under. They tried to drug me but I just wouldn't go under. Finally the obstetrician came with his forceps and yanked you out from my uterus and in that process my uterus came out partially. I am still suffering the aftermath of this difficult childbirth. Even now, once a month, my uterus comes out through my anus, did you know that?'

I didn't know what a uterus was. I only knew I was responsible for all this pain. I did not know how to make it up to her but Ma was quite clear: it was my moral duty to love her, to love her as much as she needed and wanted. I tried, even though I knew somewhere that no one would be able to love her enough, to fill the hole within her. In other words, I loved her with a love I knew was going to fail. I would always be a spoilt brat and a failure to her.

MY MOTHER WAS a college lecturer who taught philosophy to undergraduates. She wanted me to excel at academics. She wanted this so badly that she forced me to study, forced me to keep going until all interest was ground out of me.

She wanted me to be an all-rounder. Her colleagues seemed to have only paragons as children and she brought home bags full of stories about the achievements of these young geniuses. My mother saw an extraordinary singer in me. I had a good voice but she couldn't be contented with that. She wanted me to sing for her to combat her depression. She wanted me to sing a siren song, bait for her future son-in-law. She wanted me to sing so that everyone would praise her for raising her daughter so well. And so every weekend, a music tutor would arrive. I did not look forward to music lessons. I was tired from studying, from tuitions. I was miserable at missing my favourite cartoons: *Appu aur Pappu ki Kahaani, Duck Tales, Tailspin.*

And then there was dancing. I was made to learn dancing but this was not because my mother thought it might help me to win myself a husband. It was a family competition. My maternal uncle's daughter was learning kathak so it was decided that I would have to learn it too.

So that was my schedule. School every day with tuitions to follow. Then school homework, and the tuition homework. On Saturday we had a half-day at school with the final bell at one-thirty. I would return home at two, and was then dragged off to painting class at three followed by a dance class at four-thirty followed by science tuition at six-thirty. I submitted to all of these to satisfy my mother but failed miserably.

My father did not interfere. He was a renowned professor in a government degree college. He was quiet, introverted and patient. Students from other colleges flocked to him for tuitions and this angered my mother very much. She would pick a fight with my father almost every day. She would yell at him and when he retaliated she would lift her sari or petticoat and show him her privates. I was a silent spectator, my eyes filled with tears, my heart filled with a silent prayer to God, asking him to intervene and stop my mother. My God did not interfere either.

'Why are you looking at me like that?' she would ask me. 'Do you know what he plans to do? Your father, that monster, plans to kill me. Do you know what will happen when I die? He will marry someone else, some beautiful woman. And she will come here and make you her slave. She will brand you with hot coal. She will keep you hungry. Do you want me to die?'

I would hug her and beg her not to die.

But when she fought with my father and said she was going to leave the house and take me with her, I would quake with fear at the thought of being alone with her. Luckily, she never made good on those threats.

They had had an arranged marriage. My father was reluctant to marry because he had a family to support but agreed when he was told that Reema was also a college lecturer. I suppose the logic was that she was his match educationally and that she would also bring in her share of money.

My mother did earn, working for several years after her marriage. I don't know how she managed that. Perhaps she was a different person at work. And she was a good teacher. But she could never manage her expenses. Though she was a post-graduate, she could not even write a cheque on her own. The banking system was alien to her. Till her retirement, she did not know the salary she drew. She handed over her money to my father to manage and my father in return would hand her a certain amount every month for her personal use. She would save this money to spend on her siblings and their children during our visits to her mother's house after my annual exams or during the Durga Puja vacations.

But she could not be generous with them and keep herself going, so she would steal from my father. I once caught her at it.

'I know,' she said. 'Your teachers have told you that stealing is wrong.'

I nodded.

'But I am not stealing. This is not his money. This is *my* money. He takes it all and then he gives me peanuts.'

This seemed logical.

'Here, you take some too.'

This seemed like a bribe.

'Why are you hesitating? It is my money. I have taken it back and now I am giving it to you.'

It was good to have some extra money. I put aside my qualms and became her accomplice. I demonized my father: How dare he take her money away? I aligned myself with my mother: She was only taking what was hers by right. My father was not very upset by this petty thievery; he laughed it off.

My husband, many years later, did not find it funny when I stole from him. He too was mentally troubled and when he found out I was stealing from him, he responded with physical violence.

'GIVE ME A cup of tea!' my mother would yell at the help in the kitchen. She devoured around thirty cups a day and I became her tea-mate at the age of ten. To make things easier and to save fuel and labour, a huge thermos was made and my mother drank from it each time she felt like having tea.

'It calms me down,' she would say, adding some more sugar but I never found her any the calmer for it. Whenever I found a moment from my round of studies and tuitions, I would be dragged out to a neighbour's house. There my mother would demand some tea and heap it with sugar. Sugar was her substitute for serotonin, the happy hormone her brain refused to produce.

My mother was ill. She made us all aware of the fact. She had a high blood pressure problem which could not be helped by all that sugar, she had arthritis, she suffered from insomnia, but most of all, she suffered the most extraordinary agonies each month. Her menstrual cramps were legendary and she went to a series of doctors for help.

'Are you having multiple sex partners?' one of them asked her, ignoring my presence in the room.

'What is sex, Ma?' I asked her on the way home.

She told me. She told me about how my breasts would grow and how men suffered from 'nightfall'. At first, I was repulsed and uncomfortable but soon I began to be fascinated by this strange new world. I padded my dress up and looked at myself in the mirror. I was eight going on eighteen.

At that age I was introduced to both male and female genitals. Those forbidden areas were of great interest to me. My mother described herself as being 'an extremely hot-blooded mammal'. Sometimes she attributed it to her blood pressure. She also sweated excessively. To keep herself cool at home she dressed in either a plain, torn cotton sari without a blouse or petticoat; or she would tie a petticoat under her arms. I was also dressed in a thin slip or just underwear since I felt the heat too. My near-nakedness became the talk of the local boys of the small town where we stayed until I graduated; I became their local Silk Smitha. We became the 'hot' subject of idle conversation for the boys; I still remember the lusty looks I received from them when I went out. I shiver now when I recall the names they called me and the rumours that made their way back to me, carried by the malicious and the smug. My mother was aware of this but instead of getting angry or covering herself and me, she chose to ignore the situation.

She also suffered from constant vaginal itching and took no treatment; instead she would either use her fingers or a comb to ease the itching. She did this when she was alone and when I was present, as if it were a common thing to scratch, show or play with one's privates.

Even as I write this, I wonder if I am betraying her. I loved her and she betrayed me. At the age of fifteen, my science tutor began to abuse me sexually. I told my mother about this but she refused to take action. 'These things happen,' she said. I didn't think so. I couldn't imagine them happening to the other girls. And if they did, I wanted it stopped. I wanted her to stop it.

'You have to bear this if you want to get into a good engineering college,' she said.

I did get into engineering. I did graduate, and with a first class. But I also retreated into myself. I lost all self-confidence, I shied away from intimacy of any kind. My first boyfriend and I had a troubled relationship. He began to abuse drugs and me, not, I think, in that order. Many years later, I heard that he took his own life. I don't know why. I am now fighting to end a troubled marriage. I have suffered two nervous breakdowns and have begun to put my life together again. I tried psychiatry and found that pills are part of the cure; they can never be the cure. And yet, psychiatrists seem to put their faith almost entirely in these chemicals.

I lived in a haze of self-loathing. I began to believe that I was responsible for what had happened to me. I became a tragedy queen. I started believing that nothing positive could ever happen to me. That I was born to suffer and life had thrown a shadow over me.

My mother did not help much. She couldn't, of course. She was struggling herself; drowning, too. Had I tried to live with her support, I should have gone under with her.

One day, a man who tried to molest me suggested that I go and talk to a counsellor. I had no reason to trust him but I decided to give his suggestion a shot. That was how I landed up at my counsellor's place and found an atmosphere of calm and an empathetic lady who was willing to listen. I should have gone regularly but I didn't. I don't know why I didn't take counselling seriously and avoided visiting her again for a long time. Part of the problem was my mother. She branded the lady a gold-digger and warned me that she would just sit on a chair and listen.

'And then she will give you some advice. She will charge huge money for that. And for what? I can give you the same advice. Tell me your troubles,' she said.

I wanted to cry. I laughed instead and finally found a way to go back. For some reason—could it be the peace? Could it be the empathy?—I refused to listen to my mother and started to take the counselling seriously.

'She's ruining your marriage,' my mother would shout. 'Do you want to end up a sad old lonely woman?'

I looked at her. I wanted to say, 'You're the sad old woman. I'm the one who's fighting my way out.'

But I couldn't say it. I only knew that I would have to start afresh, put down old baggage, let go of my marriage, find a way to love myself. At that time, when I was travelling two hours to see my counsellor, often taking my child with me to spare her the chaos of the house; we didn't even know my mother was mentally ill.

Perhaps it was only because I confronted my own illness that I began to see that I had never had a normal mother, that she had been mentally ill for most of my life and that I had carried her into my adult life.

It was when she began to threaten my daughter that I was galvanized into action. I consulted my counsellor who listened with increasing shock to my tales of my mother. She said that she would need a psychiatrist. My father and I finally broke out of the cycle of abuse.

At this point, when my mother took her first psychiatric medicines, she was sixty-seven. The pills calmed her down but she seemed to retreat into her own world. She would no longer shout and scream; now she sat silent, staring vacantly at me and my father. My heart wept for her, was there no state in between the mania and the withdrawal? I tried all my best to keep her happy, but she seemed lost to us.

I bathed her and fed her when I could, usually on the weekends; on other days my father and the maids attended to her needs. My father sang songs to which she listened silently, showing no emotion, blinking sometimes but nothing else. I told her stories, my daughter pampered her, but she had been dragged out by a tide of chemicals. When she surfaced briefly, she would deliver a dose of unwitting pain. 'Tell God to spare me,' she murmured to me once. 'I want to live.'

I didn't know how to relay the message.

But then her heart failed her at the age of sixty-eight. The larger family wiped her memory from the collective slate. The siblings whose approval she had sought all her life forgot about her, it would seem, almost immediately after her demise. A handful of people remember her: my father, my daughter and I. Some of the domestic help who served us over the years lament her passing, remembering her incidental kindnesses. My father, always quiet, has burrowed deeper into silence. When we talk about her, he weeps.

'She was always afraid,' he said to me once. 'What was she afraid of?'

Afraid? My mother? Who lived the way she wanted? Whose inner compass determined her direction? Who told me to accept sexual abuse to get on in the world?

Two years after her death, I lie in bed sometimes and sniff the air for her smell, the smell I remember, the smell of home. And I wonder: have I forgiven?

MY MOTHER'S BREAST

Amandeep Sandhu

ALL HER LIFE, my mother, Mamman, Amarjit Kaur, had bathed at 5 a.m. That morning she could not seem to get out of bed. Our maid, Famida, went to help her and found blood on her bra.

She came and told me.

I went up to see Mamman.

'I need to look at your breast, Mamman,' I said. She nodded.

'I'm sorry but I have to do this,' I said. She nodded again.

What I saw when I raised her kurta shocked me. It was as if someone had gashed her breast and then sewn it up again, roughly. Underneath the nipple was a hole, almost an inch-and-a-half across.

'When did this happen, Mamman?' I asked.

She shrugged. She did not remember. Or she did not care to remember.

All our life together, I had been bothered about her mind. My mother lived in another world where I was the President of India, married to someone called Vivekta and, later, Harpreet. In that world, she was an invincible power, Subramaniam; she was the heiress to a fortune that ran into many crores of rupees and Rajiv Gandhi and Giani Zail Singh were paying guests in her father's home. We, the sane, called this world schizophrenia.

MY MOTHER'S BREAST

A few days before this, it had been very difficult, as always, to rouse Mamman to take her to meet Dr Naveen, her cardiologist. In January, Dr Naveen had taken an X-ray to determine some opacity in her lungs. He had prescribed diuretics. Maasi, my maternal aunt, Dr Charanjit Kaur, had also seen the X-ray when we met her in Haryana in March and she had agreed it was pleural opacity, water in the lungs. She had also wondered about 'malignancy', but when she spoke to Dr Naveen on the phone she did not bring this up. Perhaps it was professional decorum. They exchanged pleasantries and she did not probe his diagnosis or his line of treatment. Mamman had been cardiomyopathic for long. Four years ago, Dr Naveen had given her six months. But then he had also kept her going; it made sense to trust him.

Dr Naveen is a good man and had been a good doctor to Mamman, as he had been to Papa before he died. But he always sounded a little rushed. He also refused to do home visits. I had requested him to make an exception because of Mamman's schizophrenia, but he insisted that any patient who needed a home visit should be in hospital. So the morning I discovered the gash on Maman's breast, I did not call Dr Naveen. I did not have the courage to impose on him.

I mentioned Mamman's wound to my friend and colleague Cheryl and she thought of Dr Vidya, her neighbour. Dr Vidya was only twenty-seven years old. She did not have much experience but she looked at the reports with fresh eyes. She was aided by the knowledge that I had seen something on Mamman's chest. When she examined the old X-ray, her eyes lingered on something but she did not say anything.

She came home. I took her upstairs to examine Mamman.

I stood at the door of the room, behind a curtain. Dr Vidya spoke gently to Mamman and came out after some time, and I accompanied her down the steps.

She turned around and said, 'It's cancer.'

I missed my step.

Then she said, 'Maybe it's tuberculosis.' Then she looked at me again and sighed. 'No,' she said, 'it is cancer.'

She said I must go to a government hospital and get Mamman's tissue and blood culture. She said I must not go to a private hospital because they would fleece me. I began calculating immediately. Mamman had insurance worth four lakh rupees from my office, another two lakh of personal insurance, and I had credit cards that would let me spend another four lakh. Dr Vidya suggested the Kidwai Institute or the Bangalore Institute of Oncology.

That night, I wrote in my diary:

> Dr Vidya said the word just like that. With no preamble, no introduction. Just the word and the word shook my world. What shook me is that Mamman's cancer remained undetected for so long and can now cause immense pain. I do not fear Mamman's death but I am not okay with her pain. It will be pain that I cannot even imagine. I am scared. This is perhaps my scariest night. I pray that I can help Mamman handle her pain. After the doctor went away, Mamman and I listened to 'Jeena yahan, marna yahan…' It is her favourite song. She was cheerful. I hope I can build a routine around her needs.

The Kidwai Institute was on Dairy Circle, close to my office, next to the National Institute of Mental Health and Neurosciences. I had never noticed the place before. I had no need to. They confirmed what Dr Vidya had said. Cancer. Stage IV.

Dr Ramaa talked to me. She asked what Mamman's heart specialist had done if he could not see this happening. The heart and the tumour were less than six inches apart. Even if it was not part of his job, she said, he could have looked at Mamman's chest. But he hadn't. He was a man, Mamman was a woman.

She asked how I was managing. I could no longer control myself. I broke down. I could not be brave any longer. She asked me if I was married. I said my wife and I did not live together. I said for the past few months, ever since Mamman started looking weak, I had been doing everything for her, from feeding her to cheering her up. I told her: 'Mamman listens to me, she does as I ask her to do.' I told her I felt fortunate that I could take care of her so completely. But, I said, I was also tired. I told her I was scared of the pain Mamman would feel.

She said that she was the anaesthetist; it was her job to manage pain. Mamman would be under her care. She said Mamman did not need any tissue culture. If they had detected the illness earlier they could have done something. They could have surgically removed it, used chemotherapy. I responded, 'In a way, it's good we only found the illness now. Mamman wouldn't have allowed chemo. Now we can't do anything about it and Mamman need not be disfigured.'

Dr Ramaa listened quietly. 'Yes,' she said. 'Body image is important.'

Dr Ramaa asked me to get Letroz, Proxyvon, Betnosol and Pantodac. She told me the routine to administer the medicines. Our local chemist Manju could provide the medicines but had to consult with Dr Ramaa. We made three calls within five minutes but she answered patiently, with no sign of impatience or exasperation. I wanted to hug her. This is how a doctor should be: always calm, always composed, and always willing to help.

Maasi said she wanted to come and see Mamman. I replied that it wasn't possible. Enough, I felt. For years Mamman's own family had stigmatized her, kept her away when she needed them. If it had to change now, close to her end, let her sister come and take us with her to where she had her hospital. In Dabwali, on the Punjab-Haryana border, where Mamman had grown up.

The next evening I finished an office conference call downstairs and saw that Maasi had called again. She wanted to talk to Mamman. I climbed the stairs to Mamman's room. She took the mobile phone from me and the first words she spoke were a howl. A high-pitched wail of pain.

Then she shouted, 'Get him married to Harpreet.' She was gasping in pain. I told Maasi I would call her later. I held Mamman's hand and knelt down near her bed. She started removing her gold bangle and kada, trying to give them to me. 'For your wife,' she said.

'Where is the pain?' I asked.

She placed her hand on her right rib. I gently removed her hand and placed mine there. I could do nothing more. After five or maybe ten minutes the pain subsided. Mamman took my hand and kissed it. She said I was her God.

I fed Mamman and gave her the medicines. After that scream, I was never late by even a single minute. Dr Ramaa had said Proxyvon should be administered every eight hours. That kind of consistency might prevent the need for morphine.

I wrote to my managers, telling them I might have to leave for

Punjab. 'I hope the company can use my services.' My managers decided not to let their higher-ups know I was going to work remotely and allowed me to leave.

In the days between the scream and our leaving, I stabilized Mamman on Proxyvon. Dr Ramaa was considering whether we should start morphine. These days morphine comes as an oral pill but very few hospitals issue it. I would have had to register Mamman with the Kidwai Institute. I could not even think of admitting Mamman to a hospital, she would have resisted it vehemently. Dr Ramaa decided to give me a letter to a doctor in the Post-Graduate Institute of Medical Education and Research, Chandigarh. She said in case all the medicines stopped working I could get morphine from there.

Maasi came on 4th May. Before I left, Cheryl got me to sign a whole bunch of cheques to manage my accounts. She loaded the laptop with all necessary programmes and accesses. The laptop was now my complete office.

At the airport, Sahara Airlines wanted a certificate declaring Mamman fit to travel. I did not understand. I tried to tell them that Maasi was a doctor and she was accompanying us. They were not interested. They only needed Maasi's letterhead. We could not supply that. I asked the booking clerk what he would do if his mother were ill.

'Please don't mention my mother,' he snapped but gave me a declaration form to fill.

Once we signed a declaration that we would not sue the airline if anything happened to Mamman, the airline staff calmed down and were very good to us. They arranged for a wheelchair, gave us special security clearance, and an early entry into the airplane. The booking clerk came up and told me that his mother also suffered from cancer.

IN DABWALI, I began to understand Maasi and Mamman. I began to understand the complexities of their relationship. Their mother had passed away early, before Maasi joined medical school. Mamman had brought up Maasi. Young Mamman had plaited Maasi's hair, cooked her food, organized her clothes, attended to all her needs. Mamman was proud that her kid sister was becoming a doctor. Later, after the discovery of Mamman's mental illness and subsequent marriage to my father, they had drifted apart.

Mamman was not happy with her marriage, she would ask Nanaji and then Maasi to take her away, back to Punjab. I still remember the cold winter night when Nanaji had thrown us out of the Dabwali home. Maasi had not intervened. Mamman and I had spent the night shivering at Bhatinda station.

Once, when I was young, Mamman waited for seven years to hear from Maasi. Every afternoon, summer, winter, rains, she paced the garden in front of our house in Rourkela. Over the last two years in Bangalore she would call Maasi every weekend and ask her to take her to Punjab. It irritated me. Perhaps it hurt me too. I did not want Mamman to call Maasi. I did not want her to beg Maasi to help us. Last year, when I went to the US for three weeks, I left Mamman with her brother in Patiala. I stopped contact with Maasi for months.

Now, Maasi started combing Mamman's hair. She recalled the time when Mamman would do this for her. We got Mamman new clothes, salwars with elasticized belts, easier to slip on and remove.

MY MOTHER'S BREAST

I realized, in my heart, that I had judged Maasi harshly. She'd had her share of troubles. Widowed early, she had no children, and after Nanaji died she had no support. She had fought hard to build her medical practice. Watching her spend time with Mamman in between her demanding hospital work, I understood why she always said she could keep Mamman provided I stayed on to take care of her. Even if Maasi had wanted to she could not have spared too much time for Mamman. She was busy with her patients, some of whom came to her at any time of the day and night, and many of whom could not afford other private hospitals. And in the end, Mamman was my responsibility, after all, not Maasi's.

One of the biggest issues Maasi and I faced was Mamman's constipation. Palliative care literature will tell you that one of the certain side effects of medication for cancer is constipation. I told Maasi, who had also noticed a bulge in Mamman's tummy. She organized gloves and buckets and we started giving Mamman mild laxatives. Maasi did not mind cleaning Mamman. She cleans her dog Sheru's poo; she administers enemas to her patients. Still, initially Maasi recoiled at Mamman's condition. I think Mamman's constipation had been building up over months. After Mamman passed away and I returned to Bangalore I discovered that Mamman's bathroom flush did not work on full pressure. She would have had to pour a bucket of water after going to the toilet. I think ever since Mamman could not pick up the bucket she started avoiding going to the toilet. And then I remembered—many a time in the last few months Mamman took medicine for dysentery if she ever happened to go to the toilet twice a day.

When I saw Maasi recoil, I had half a mind to take Mamman away. Then I saw Mamman's expression after she passed a stool. It said: Well, this is what it is, I cannot help it. That expression undid my ego. I think it also spoke to Maasi. After that, we participated in that one activity which is most shameful for both the patient and the caregiver in absolute silence.

Now our common intention was to help Mamman; when we were with her, it was all that occupied our minds. To me, I think it was a way of blocking the feeling of complete helplessness. Uselessness. First her mental illness, now cancer; she had always suffered alone. Once when Maasi saw me washing Mamman's soiled salwar she gave up trying to tell me to not participate in her care. Before that she would say it was work for a girl. I would say I was a daughter to Mamman.

That is what we became, genderless. We dressed Mamman, helped Mamman to the potty, bathed her. I carried a naked Mamman to and from the bathroom and Maasi gave her baths.

Mamman could trust us. We were her Gods. And she was ours. Serving her was our life. It was our penance.

ONE NIGHT, MAMMAN fell asleep around eleven. I was working on my computer. I came and lay down next to her, watching her. I saw Mamman's body becoming stiff. Her face started contorting, becoming darker. She threw away the sheet covering her and her arms started bending at unusual angles. I sat up in bed. My ears were attuned to her breathing. The oxygen pipe slipped from her nose. I put it back again. Her legs started bending, she started to turn. I gently pushed her back into the position where the oxygen pipe was most comfortable. Her body kept twisting and soon she became unrecognizable.

MY MOTHER'S BREAST

I stood up next to her, stepped back, came close, and kept watching her. I do not know if this is an appropriate way of saying this: she started looking like an abject beggar, homeless, destitute, and sick.

In the last few days Mamman and I had started reciting the mool mantar together. It was not out of a sense of religion. It was more a custom. Once, when I was a teenager, I had asked Mamman why she did not pray. 'Why should I pray? What has God given me?' she had said. But in the last two years of her life she had started to listen to gurbani and kirtan broadcast live from the Golden Temple. I do not think Mamman ever analyzed the lines. When we did the mool mantar, I always led the recitation. Maasi had given me a compact disc of Nit Nem and I played it in the morning before I played Mamman songs from her favourite cassette. From time to time I also played the Sukhmani Sahib on tape.

That night, I think I recited the mool mantar as I watched Mamman in silent agony. Was it something terrible in her mind again, or was it a physical pain?

Slowly, as the night waned, Mamman got back her looks. By morning she started looking as she was when she had gone to sleep. I covered her. I did not speak about what I had seen.

A day after the night episode I was sitting at my table at four in the evening when Mamman asked for another khes, a cotton rug. I thought she might be a little cold and gave her the khes. I checked her temperature. It was fine. Her breathing was normal. I went back to working when Mamman asked for a blanket. I went out of the room, found Prem, Maasi's Man Friday, and asked him for a blanket. Prem found a warm blanket. He and I put that on Mamman. I switched off the cooler. I asked Prem to call Maasi. He said the priests from the Chor Mar Sahib Gurudwara had come and Maasi was attending to them.

I did not know how to make Mamman warm. I started massaging her feet. She was not getting any warmth. I started massaging her hands. She was still feeling cold. I wondered if this was how death came, like a chill. I had seen Papa just after he passed away. He did not say anything; he was cold, yet his breath vanished slowly while he was in my hands. I thought I was seeing the chill invade Mamman.

Suddenly the room door opened and I saw a priest. Maasi was with him and introduced him as Bhai Gurpal Singh. He was tall, angular-faced, and had a certain serenity. I turned towards him, still holding Mamman's hand, and asked him if he could pray. I could think of nothing more holy than prayers when Mamman was leaving her body. The Guru Granth Sahib is a collection of beautiful poetry by poets and saints who mused upon life and living. What could be better than reciting their pure words when someone was dying? He asked what prayers. I said Japuji Sahib. He said this was not the time for that. I said anything, Sukhmani Sahib, or just the mool mantar.

He quickly went to the bathroom to wash his hands and feet and came back. In the Sikh tradition we cannot not have any person at a level higher than the level from where the prayers are recited. Knowing that Mamman could not get up, Bhai Gurpal Singh climbed on to the double bed and sat down cross-legged. He started reciting the mool mantar, and a bit of the Japuji Sahib. Maasi sat on a chair, Prem stood at the door. I covered my head with a towel and knelt down next to Mamman, crying and rubbing her hands. Bhai Gurpal Singh recited the prayers for ten minutes. That time, for me, was a period of total acceptance of what might happen.

MY MOTHER'S BREAST

In those minutes Mamman's face started regaining colour. When Bhaiji finished, I asked Mamman how she was feeling. She said she was fine. I asked if she was cold. She said no, I could remove the blanket. She said Sat Sri Akal to Bhaiji. I touched his feet.

What was this? Did God come to save Mamman? I feel it was the power of recitation, of centering your thoughts. Some power, maybe God, was showing me how we can centre ourselves to rise above our maladies.

MAMMAN'S BACK HAD started perforating. She had also started developing rashes under her wound, though the hole itself had almost closed. While we were at Dabwali, a patient of Maasi's complained about pain in the breast. Maasi immediately referred her for mammography. It turned out the woman had breast cancer and the doctors operated on her. Later, she came to Maasi to get her breast dressed. Maasi said that Mamman's laceration seemed exactly like that woman's who had undergone surgery.

We got Mamman's chest X-rayed and found the fluid in her lungs was rising. We had done another test to find her CA 15-3 protein levels. CA 15-3 protein is a marker of the extent of breast cancer. The normal range is between 0.5 and 32; Mamman's reading was 265. But she did not feel any pain; at least she said she had no pain.

What prevented that pain? Was it God, in whom she did not believe?

I know a story. There were a priest and a robber. The priest prayed to God every day and every day the robber came and slapped the idol of God with his slippers. On days when it rained or if it was too hot, the priest did not pray but the robber never missed a single day. Finally when God appeared, he appeared to the robber and not the priest. Was Mamman's steadfast refusal to acknowledge God so great that God had intervened and helped her? I do not know. Still there is the matter of Mamman's cancerous breast vanishing and she not feeling any pain. Did God think that she had suffered enough in the labyrinths of her mind? Or was her schizophrenia allowing her the distance?

On 21st May Mamman developed crepitation, a rattling sound in the lungs. After that every morning we spent hours reviving Mamman. Finally, we kept the oxygen on twenty-four hours and started feeding Mamman while she lay on the bed. In those days, every time it happened, Maasi and her attendants tried out these things: a nebulizer, injections to raise or reduce blood pressure, and an oral drop for the heart. It seemed to me that if these were the only weapons we humans had evolved over the last couple of thousand years to fight death, we had followed a very false trajectory of evolution.

On the morning of 28th May we found it hard to revive Mamman. We tried injections, nebulizer, drops, everything, but Mamman would not open her eyes. Maasi even brought the holy water from the sarovar at Amritsar and touched it to Mamman's eyelids and put some in her mouth. After some time Mamman opened her eyes. It had taken us six hours.

That afternoon, at around four, Mamman said she wanted to go to the bathroom. For the last couple of days we had encouraged Mamman to urinate and even defecate on the bed on plastic sheets. I had often changed her in the middle of night. But Mamman now forced herself to sit up and asked me to help her to the bathroom.

I removed her oxygen tube and half-carried her to the toilet seat. When she finished, I helped Mamman to the bed. I fixed her nebulizer and felt she was not responding to my call. I ran down and saw Maasi had not yet got into the operating theatre. I called her.

Maasi came up and checked Mamman's blood pressure. It had fallen. She quickly arranged for an injection and while she was treating Mamman she started berating me. Her words were harsh. She had panicked.

Everything came out. She scolded me for not discovering Mamman's cancer soon enough. She scolded me for never having done enough for Mamman, for not holding on to my marriage. She scolded me for not having a woman in my life who could have looked after Mamman. She scolded me for letting Mamman go to the toilet. Most of all she scolded me for caring for Mamman's needs as if I were alone while I was with her, for not letting her, Maasi, participate even when she was right there, next to her own sister.

Finally, I gave in to anger. I started speaking back. I said I did not know of another way but to be alone. I had done my best, she had done her best, but where was she or anybody else for the whole of Mamman's life? Mamman yearned for love but no one would give it to her. I said that as soon as I could earn I got both Mamman and Papa to live with me. I saw to it that Papa fulfilled his wishes before he died; I was seeing to it that Mamman fulfilled her wishes. There had been no one and there would be no one after I left Dabwali. Then I walked out of the room.

I paced the courtyard, calming myself, and it occurred to me that the last month had been the most fulfilling for Mamman, but it did not take away from the fact that Mamman had been neglected by her own and Papa's family all her life. Did that mean that all that had happened in the last month was false? No, I thought to myself: no, it does not mean that. The period before the month was true and this month is also true. The period in the future will be true. All truth exists. All of it exists simultaneously. Each moment contains in it the truth of the past, present and future.

I came back. Mamman had urinated again. I called Maasi. I let her change Mamman. She was doing it badly because her hands were trembling. I helped her. We saw Mamman had also defecated. We cleaned her up. I cried. I apologized to Maasi. Maasi told me my anger was the same as it was when I was a child.

That night Maasi and I both fed Mamman together. In some ways the outburst had relaxed us. Our poison drawn, we became lighter. But we forgot that Mamman had heard everything. I think it did something to her. I remember a few days before Papa passed away I had scolded him. Papa had called me at the office saying he wanted to get new sofa covers. I said we must wait. He did not listen and started shouting at me. I had to raise my voice and silence him. In a few days I got new sofa covers made, but Papa saw them only once. He passed away soon after that. He died of cardiac arrest. Mamman also died of cardiac arrest. Both their hearts collapsed but my anger broke their hearts before they collapsed.

I am not beating myself up for what happened but I do realize that anger is a destructive force. I also realize that anger, when it comes from the tongue, is most destructive. If I do not learn this now, I will never learn it.

Early morning on May 29th, I gave Mamman some tea with a spoon, and then her medicines. By this time Mamman was on twenty-two tablets and her doctors said each of them was necessary.

MY MOTHER'S BREAST

When Papa had hit thirteen tablets I had sensed something was wrong. Now Mamman was on twenty-two, plus the laxative and sometimes injections. Cheryl said that twenty-two tablets were like a complete lunch. I wondered why we do not have combination medicines for the aged.

So Maasi and I had started on a new way of administering the pills: crushing them and giving them in powder form. It was such a simple idea to crush her tablets, but it never occurred to me earlier. That is what we need when we provide care: simple and effective ideas. There was still so much to learn.

That morning Mamman asked for tea thrice. The third time, at around 10.30, I told her to wait until my father's family came from Rajpura; they had called to say they wanted to visit her. Finally, my father's family came: Chachaji, Phuphadji, Mummyji, Manju Bhabhiji and Lali Veerji. Mamman talked to each one, she even asked about Manju Bhabhi's daughter Muskaan. I fed Mamman tea again. We talked some more. I tried to feed daal and roti to Mamman. She could not eat much. I asked Maasi to feed her. I sat down for lunch with the others. Maasi was feeding Mamman inside. Just when I was finishing lunch, and the others were about to eat the mangoes, Maasi called me to Mamman's room.

Mamman was gasping for breath. An attendant was trying to give her an injection. Maasi was standing near Mamman, holding her hand. She was crying. I thought I heard Mamman say 'chah'. Tea. Or maybe desire. Then she was quiet. I went close to Mamman. I waved to the attendant to stop the injection. Mamman had begun her journey into peace. I started saying that I was proud she was my mother, that I had not seen her kind of courage in anyone, that she had been a truly brave daughter of her father, that I was the President of India, that I had learnt so much from her, that she and I had had a wonderful life, and Papa had worked hard to ensure we got that life. Mamman was almost without breath. She opened her eyes and I started reciting the mool mantar. I told her Maasi and I were with her. We loved her.

Mamman passed away. It was 2.15 p.m.

MAASI, MANJU BHABHI and I bathed Mamman. We dressed her. Maasi had readied clothes for Mamman and me. The sun was to set at 7.30 p.m. We planned the cremation on the same day.

Bhai Gurpal Singh said the prayers. I stayed back until the funeral pyre went out. Workers from Maasi's farm helped with the cremation. Half an hour after the pyre was lit, one of them said that Mamman's skull had burst. The head which had confused the world, the head which was Mamman's prison, had finally released her.

Mamman had wanted to die in her real home, in Punjab, and in the presence of Papa's family. I remember scenes from my childhood, when this family treated Mamman like an animal. They would beat her and lock her in a room. Mamman had forgotten that. Or maybe she thought she deserved it because of her mental illness. That Mummyji, Papa's elder brother's wife, and now the head of the family, had come to meet her was important to Mamman. In a way Mummyji released Mamman.

I slept fitfully that night. I dreamt that I was back at nursery school. I was standing at the gate. The mothers of all the other children had come and taken them. I was waiting for Mamman. She had not come.

The next morning we picked the phul—flowers, an euphemism

for bones. We placed them in the locker of the cremation ground. In the afternoon we took the ashes of the wood to a canal close by. When we emptied the gunnysack I saw the ashes spreading out in the canal in the form of a human body. The arms stretched to the sides, the body horizontal. The shape in the canal looked like how Mamman was when we picked the sheet off her and took her for her last bath, before her funeral.

I was unable to close my eyes for a moment from the time I picked the phul, the flowers, until we reached Haridwar and immersed them in the Ganga. And when I finally closed my eyes I saw horrible things: Mamman's body being cut in the middle, a pile of faeces next to her pyre, and so on. Maasi and I immersed the flowers at the very same place where Mamman and I had immersed Papa's flowers. In my mind I sang 'Jeena yahaan, marna yahaan', just like I had sung Madhushala for Papa. I looked at the river waters and I do not know if it was an apparition but I saw two silver fishes swimming away.

I CAME BACK to Bangalore. I picked up my car from my friend's home and drove to the house. I opened the door and went upstairs. Famida had not touched Mamman's room. I had told her not to. I lay down on Mamman's bed. A few days before Mamman passed away I had dreamt that I had returned to this house and was sleeping in Papa's room, which after him I had made my own. Mamman was calling me from her bed, the way she used to in her last days in Bangalore. I dreamt that I could not get up. Her cries became more insistent. In my dream I felt I would go crazy.

Every day I wake up and have my breakfast. I leave home, I work,

LEELA CHAKRAVORTY

I return in the evening. Famida cooks the dinner. I have taken out some old photographs. I will blow them up and put them up on the walls. I don't know how long I will live in this house. Someday I will leave and never return.

MOTHERS AND DAUGHTERS

Nirupama Dutt

I COULD EASILY write a thesis on mothers and daughters because I have had so many mothers. Never a father. I suppose there must have been one but I didn't see him. I only remember a frail, fair woman holding me to her breast. She wept silently all the time. Even when I suckled her, I would see tears rolling down her pale cheeks. Who was she, this lady with the river of tears running down her cheeks? Now when I look back, I think the best way to describe her would be Mother Number 1. This is not qualitative but chronological because I was to have many mothers. This weepy one was the first and we were together precisely for ten months: nine months in her tummy and one in her lap.

I have memories that go back to my time in that womb. Of course you won't believe this. It's all right, she's not normal, you will say. You won't say this to my face. But you should. I would prefer it to your clumsy kindness.

When I was inside that frail woman, she did not weep, but something went wrong just as I wriggled out. Her father-in-law, the grandfather of that house, cried out in anger: 'What has she given birth to? Tatti? She is the ruin of my son and our family. Destroy this filth, kill her!' All the women in the village house trembled and Mother Number 1 shut her eyes in pain and fear.

It was not a nice thing to be greeted as a piece of shit. But I should not take it personally, because this happens in Haryana all the time. There, for hundreds of years, a girl child has been referred to as tatti. Shit. Before those machines were invented, the machines that can show you the dim outline of a child and its genitals, many newborn girls were given the extract of poisonous plants or opium, or they were smothered with pillows or wet blankets. But the machines were in use by the time I was born. So it must have been the money. Or the bother of finding a doctor with the machine.

The day I turned a month old, Mother Number 1 dressed me in a pink frock, wrapped me in two sweaters and a yellow knitted cap. She wept some more and then her mother-in-law pulled me away from her breast and handed me to the white-haired midwife with a black shawl wrapped around her head and shoulders. She seemed scary, this woman, and I would harbour a fear of white-haired women with shawls through much of my babyhood. It was a cold evening. As the old woman carried me out of the house, the grandfather was raving and ranting in the courtyard about the sluts, by which he meant the women of the house, who had already taken too long to get rid of the tatti. I did not want to leave Mother Number 1. I did not want to be called tatti. I did not want to be carried by the white-haired woman. I tried howling but she pressed me to her ample chest and her flesh swallowed my screams. It would not be the last time a woman would try, in vain, to absorb my grieving.

She walked a long distance to the next village where there was a railway station and we got into a nearly empty slow-moving train.

MOTHERS AND DAUGHTERS

It was dark. The old woman opened a window. A draught of chilly air rushed in. It was mid-December and dreadfully cold. The old woman picked me up and threw me out of the moving train. The train chugged on without a care and I lay, mercifully unconscious, on a parallel track.

I must have slept silently through the night because no cats and dogs got to me, but the next morning I must have howled for milk because I heard footsteps approaching and when I opened my eyes two tall Haryanvi policemen were bending over me. They took me to the nearest town hospital and registered a medico-legal case. Two days later I was taken to an ashram. Later I was told that I had reached with my right eye popping out and a badly scraped back. But I was alive. This piece of shit was not easy to kill. Two advertisements were put in two newspapers about my discovery but no one came forward to claim me.

I became the youngest addition to the girls' enclosure of the ashram. There were a lot of girls, girls of all ages, and all of us slept in one long room. Enter, at this point, Mother Number 2. I don't know how it happened but an eleven-year-old girl who was what they call deaf-and-dumb took a fancy to me. Perhaps I reminded her of her younger sister who was in the village home with the parents. Sumitra, that was the name of the girl, spoke no evil and heard no evil. She had been sent to the ashram to study in a school for the challenged. Sumitra started carrying me around, feeding me milk from a small bottle and cleaning me when I soiled myself. No one asked her to do this; she liked doing it. A few months later she would take me out of the cradle and I would sleep with this little mother of mine in her bed. The Lady Superintendent had named me Prerna, or inspiration. I don't know what was so inspiring about me; perhaps it was my survival instinct. But how I had survived and what had not survived was revealed many years later.

I was quite happy in the ashram, with Sumitra playing mother, but then the unexpected entry of Mother Number 3 changed everything. This one had tired of the fruitless romances she had had in her twenties and, feeling deprived of motherhood, she wished to adopt a child. Having had a brush with both feminism and communism and being politically correct, she told the ashram that she would not choose a child but simply adopt the youngest girl child available with them. But she did end up 'choosing', after all. I know this for a fact because I was not the youngest girl child in the ashram. Thin sickly Anu, eight months old, was the youngest, but the Superintendent, who was also the elder sister of Mother Number 3, advised her against adopting such a frail child. I was two months older than Anu and a hardy little thing. My fair face and brown hair might also have affected her decision. And I know that my droopy eye pleased her because she herself had what they call a sexy squint. She was also a 'menti-sental' type who had had a doll in her childhood with eyes that opened when it was vertical and closed when it was horizontal, but the mechanism had gone wrong in one eye and it drooped. I reminded her of that doll. But if she thought she was taking a little doll home, she was sadly mistaken.

Sumitra spoke to me in sign language and by the time I left the ashram, I had mastered this language and preferred it to baby noises. People at the ashram and, later, Mother Number 3's friends wondered if I would ever speak. But I did speak one day in sheer agony when Number 3 was heartless enough to take me to a barber in Chandigarh. There she had to hold me down as I howled while the barber ruthlessly shaved my lovely brown hair off to help the louse-bitten sores on my scalp heal. I came back home, stood in front of the tall mirror in the bedroom and wept some more and cried out my first word, twice: 'Baal! Baal!' Adding insult to injury, awful Number 3 laughed and said, 'See what it has taken to make her speak!'

Make me speak indeed! Little did she realize how well my brown hair and fair skin and chubby cheeks had served me. All the girls in the ashram vied with one another to carry me in spite of my drooping lazy right eye. Anyway, I wore a bonnet for some months, the hair came back, but I never stopped speaking.

But we are getting ahead of the story. One thing is clear: I did not choose Mother Number 3. It was her need and not mine. Once the decision had been taken both Sumitra and I were moved from the dorm to the home of the Lady Superintendent, who was my maasi, and gifts started arriving for me. The adoption process took some eight months and Number 3 would come every other month with clothes and toys. I didn't much care for them, except the two pairs of socks, for I had never worn anything on my feet. I was frankly irritated when the girls left me with her saying, 'Teri Mummyji aa gayi!' But all was not bad; a pleasant surprise came along with this new mother one day. This was a grandmother with short white hair—but no black veil, so I was not scared of her. She had a comforting smell, warm and a little musty. I like to call her Mother Number 4. She was the best of the lot, but it ended much too soon.

That's the problem with grandmothers. One never knows when.

That day I allowed this grandmother to carry me out of the ashram for the first time. There were other people too, I remember, and Number 3, of course. We went to some office and papers were signed; sweets were distributed to all the children at the ashram after the evening prayers. I enjoyed the attention. Early the next morning I was in a train to Chandigarh with mother and grandmother. I chose to ignore the former and let the latter show me the sights outside the window. For some reason I had no fear of trains, which is strange considering I was flung out of one. Let us not dwell on this mystery, let us return to our story. In the train I thought I was going for an outing and would be back in the ashram with Sumitra at night, but that was not to be.

I was taken to a town-house facing the market. Here, a new kind of life began with the two ladies and a man who said I should call him 'Uncle'. One day I did something quite wicked. It was raining and I was not well. Mother Number 3 took me to the little verandah and started showing me the rain. What was the big deal about rain? Why had she brought me out when she could see I was coughing and the light hurt my eyes? And why was she cooing stupidly in my face? I felt so angry that I gave her a tight slap. Uncle laughed. But Number 3 said there was something wrong, I had a fever and I was shaking. I got worse and the doctor said it was measles. Number 3 took leave from her office to look after me. It was then that I started accepting her a little. She was not fair like me or Mother Number 4, my grandmother, but I began to realize that brown people can be nice too.

I got admission in the best nursery school but trouble started soon after because I could not do simple tasks like the other children, I was sometimes incontinent and I just could not write the numeral 2. The nuns called Mother Number 3 and said there was some problem. This made Number 3 furious and she blamed it on the heartless education system where there was one teacher for fifty students. I was moved to another school which had sandpits to play in and different ways of teaching. But somehow I was always a little behind the other children. One day the Big Madam of the school told us not to shout but everyone kept shouting so I gave them all a tight slap each and they stopped playing with me.

Later I did make some friends and we went together to school in a rickshaw. I think I was six when I started hearing some children in the rickshaw say that Number 3 was not married, how come she had a child? I thought it was time to do some plain speaking.

I went home and said: 'You fool, didn't you know that you had to marry first and then go to the hospital to get me?'

You see, by then I had forgotten all about the toss from the train, the ashram and the two mothers before her.

Number 3 was ready to explain. I bet she had expected this and had already consulted sundry psychologists to get her act together. After all, she was a great believer in those things. She also put me through the rigmarole of psychologists and psychiatrists, brain mapping and IQ tests, besides those scary eye operations for many years. Now she put her arm around me and said that there are two ways of having children: one was to bring them out of the tummy and the other to adopt them.

'In our case I adopted you.'

My face fell and I asked her upfront: 'Why could you not bring me out of your tummy?'

'Because I was not married and I wanted a child badly. So I adopted you. It is the same thing.'

She looked so sad when she said it that I decided to let her be and offering her my hand said, 'Promise me that you have adopted me!'

'I promise you.'

Back then I did not quite know what adoption was but I believed her. I held on to the fact that she had wanted me badly. I used it too: I could get my way with her. Anyway, she was one of those coolie-type people; always running errands for me, my grandmother and many others. And my grandmother was always on my side and made sure I got all that I wanted.

I had Number 3 where I wanted her.

IF THINGS WENT right it was because my grandmother and I had something to do with it; if something went wrong it was all the fault of this Number 3. If she tried to stop me from doing something or corrected me, I would promptly tell her: 'But my Mother Number 1 who brought me out from her tummy would have let me do it'. You should have seen how her face would fall, and she would do anything then to please me. I realized that she would go through life trying to please me so I had only to pout my lips, wrinkle my nose or even raise an eyebrow to get what I wanted.

I was two months short of my ninth birthday when something terrible happened. It was an evening in September. Grandmother was helping me with my spellings. Number 3 had gone to the market to get some pickle as my two aunts had come from Delhi and there was no pickle at home to serve with the dinner. Suddenly Grandmother's head dropped to her chest and she sank to one side on the settee. We tried to shake her but we got no response. I ran to the market and found Number 3 at the grocer's and started hitting her, crying, 'Here you are buying pickles and Grandmother is ill!'

The doctor was called but Grandmother was never the same again. She lost her speech and could only mumble. She started walking after two weeks but after a few months she fell and was bedridden. But she still managed to show her love and I enjoyed spending time with her. In the middle of all this Number 3 decided to move to Delhi with Grandmother and me. I did not like leaving Chandigarh but Number 3 felt that her career as a journalist and writer would prosper in Delhi and it would be better for all of us. For a while there was no school in Delhi and a new neighbourhood. By then I had forgotten the adoption story so I wanted to know all over again about the missing father and the mother who brought me out of her tummy. I was given a story about a rail accident that had taken my parents and left me. My real story was softened because the psychologist felt that I would not be able to handle the truth about my abandonment. I was also told that all this happened somewhere near a town called Hisar in Haryana. It so happened that a family from Hisar lived in our apartment block and I started spending a lot of time at their house. I felt an affinity with them, as though they might have known my real parents. Then I started giving my costly possessions—new books, games, trinkets—to the children of the Hisar family. This would annoy my maasi, who was quite a dragon and was staying with us to help out with Grandmother.

Grandmother needed help with every small thing. Seeing her like this hurt me deeply. You see, with mothers there is always a problem about which one brought you out of her tummy and which one did not, but with grandmothers there is no such problem. You are always safe in a grandmother's heart. She could no longer talk or chase me around but she loved me and if Number 3 ever said anything nasty to me or tried to check me, she would shake her finger and make sure that I was not scolded. Grandmother and I had a game when we wanted to irritate Number 3 who would be gathering her news stories on the telephone because she couldn't go to too many places. We would start bleating like sheep, 'Baah, baah, baah,' at the top of our voices. Sometimes Number 3 would bang the phone down and start weeping in exasperation. It was good to see that big strong woman shedding tears like a baby. Happily, mobile phones had not yet come to India or she would have locked herself in the loo to do her interviews and paid no heed to the mad sheep in her fold.

Once again, in Delhi, Number 3 had to find a school for me. She had to get me assessed. I overheard a cousin telling Number 3, 'Don't be in denial. It is not just the eye or hand-eye coordination. It is evident that it's more. Please treat a problem like a problem.' I wondered what or who was the problem. And was there one problem or more? Was I a problem or was Number 3 a problem? I took more written tests, this time with an awful lady who kept saying 'borderline IQ'. Now I did not know what this wretched IQ was but I gathered it led to a learning disability and what they called 'errors in judgement'.

Number 3 was very happy when she found Educare, a remedial school for learning-disorder types. The school was nice and so were the teachers. Here each class had six to eight children and we were taught in ways I had not experienced before. I learned to read and write well and with two double promotions I was in Class VIII in three years. I had friends and Number 3 took me to fancy functions and parties. I don't know how she knew so many people and why people liked her so much. I would tell her bluntly: 'If you weren't working for a newspaper no one would talk to you.' Or I would say, 'If I was not at the party with you, you would not have had anyone to talk to.' I noticed my Number 3 stayed in the shadows at weddings of cousins while I liked to be in the forefront. At one wedding she went out to smoke while the ceremony was on. When I went out to see where she was, she said, 'I get a little bored with these long wedding ceremonies.'

This made me angry and I retorted, 'You are saying this because you are not married yourself!'

I said nasty things because I was very hurt that she did not bring me out of her tummy. This chocolate brown mother was not bad but she had to be kept in control.

And then the most terrible thing happened. Actually, Number 3 had been trying to tell me for some time that Grandmother's time had come, but I never believed her. One day she came from her work to pick me up at my school. We rushed home and there was Grandmother lying on her bed all blue in the face, eyes open and breathing heavily. Number 3 rushed her to the hospital and I was at home. I remember I was asked to share a dosa with an older cousin.

And then the news came. I learned what death was for the first time and that too the death of my favourite person. I hated the face of the hospital boy who came with this awful information. I felt that I was no longer safe in anyone's heart.

Number 3 was different now. Through much of my life when I needed her around me, she was out on the terrace or the lawn, depending on what was available, smoking a cigarette. Now she would not leave me alone, fussing and watching over me day and night. Her behaviour became worse when we returned to Chandigarh. I was all of eighteen and started making male friends. She found no one good enough because she said they were dangerous, too old or 'exploitative'. She insisted that one boy on a bike who followed me was a girl and not a boy. Then in a couple of years she started looking for boys for me to get married to. But I was determined to find a boy myself just as my cousins and childhood friends were doing. Once she brought a boy who distributed books for a living to see me. He was good-looking and earned well but I had a nagging suspicion that Number 3 had chosen him because he would distribute her own books, and that too for free. Books were her world and I hated them.

Finally, I did find someone who she thought I could marry. And what a great wedding it was, but things that followed were not so great.

In all fairness she did not go out to smoke during my wedding and later she was there when I needed her, which I did most of the time because my husband was strange. He too had had a bump on his head in his childhood but he was always making me feel that he had done me a favour by marrying me.

'You duffer!' he would say to me. 'You filth of the gutter!'

When Number 3 fretted about me to her other single friends, my maasis, they told her: 'Don't worry. Prerna is a survivor, she'll get through in life. She has already accomplished more than we did—a husband and a child out of her tummy!'

When my daughter was brought out from the gash in my tummy, I was overjoyed. My husband and his family would have wanted a baby boy but I was very happy with a baby girl. I have been careful that she never gets hurt, for I know what it is to manage life with ruptured nerves. I did it but my daughter will never have to do it. Daughters have to be brought up with care, not chucked around and left with disabilities.

When Mother Number 3 came to the labour room after my daughter came out squealing, I somehow felt good about all

MOTHERS AND DAUGHTERS

mothers and daughters. Mercy that there was no crazy old man around ranting about tatti. 'Go have a look at your grand-daughter!' I told Number 3 but I also wanted to tell her that I had brought this daughter out of my tummy and I would always keep her out of harm's way. She was my gift to Number 3, straight from my tummy.

Number 3, you are a granny now. You are a granny who smokes on terraces but you are a granny. May my little one be safe in your heart always!

DANIELLA

Patricia Mukhim

IT WAS ON a January afternoon in 2006 that I first heard the term 'bipolar disorder'. I was in a park inside the American University campus at Ardmore, Pennsylvania. There was a pond located in what looked like a botanical garden, a charming recreational space for parents who came with their kids to feed the ducks. Young lovers sat on the less-frequented side, whispering sweet nothings. I was grateful for the unusually warm weather, although I knew it could all change in an hour and we might be snowed in the next morning. I was in the US for a sabbatical, supported by an organization that wanted me to write a book on the Khasi matrilineal society to which I belong. After a long day at the university library, it was good to sit in the shade of the trees that circled the pond, watching the children play. Then, as I was about to leave the park, I saw a young Chinese-American woman standing by the water. She seemed to be talking to herself. I stopped and began to watch her. After a while I saw her weeping. She muttered and wept, mopping her eyes from time to time.

On an impulse, I decided to offer her a shoulder to cry on.

'Hi, my name is Patricia,' I began.

DANIELLA

She looked at me, but did not say anything. At least she didn't turn away.

'I'm from India,' I ploughed on. 'I'm here on sabbatical. I come here every evening.'

She hiccupped.

'Do you live here?'

'I'm Yang,' she said finally. 'I come to feed the ducks. It's so peaceful here.'

I agreed that it was and we stood together in silence. After a while she said, 'They eat what I give them. They don't taunt me.'

'Taunt you? But why would anyone do that?' I asked.

'My boyfriend told me to find a psychiatrist because he said I throw too many tantrums. The psychiatrist said I have bipolar disorder.'

My confusion must have been evident because she explained. 'It's a mental disorder,' she said. 'Mood swings. One day you're happy, the next day you want to die.'

I nodded.

'My boyfriend has left me because he says he can't deal with it,' she sobbed. 'I'm so in love with him. I thought he loved me too…'

I wanted to hug her but wasn't sure how she would take it.

'Why don't we sit down for a bit?' I said.

As Yang told me about her life, I cast about for what I should be saying. I remembered a talk given by an Australian psychiatrist, Anne Stroh, in Shillong. She had come to Meghalaya at the invitation of a non-governmental organization, the Initiatives of Change (IofC, formerly the Moral Rearmament). 'Listen with empathy,' Anne had said. 'The person with depression needs someone to talk to. She does not need advice. No unsolicited advice. Depressed people don't need it. They need an active, empathic ear.'

Depression had recently become a much-mentioned word in Shillong. Psychiatrist friends would tell me that young people were increasingly prone to it and yet there were very few health workers in this area and very little awareness. Perhaps, like me, most people only talked about depression among the young, never really confronting the problem. If we talked about it, we didn't have to listen.

That January evening in a distant country, Yang told me about herself, her family, her education and her love life. But as she talked, I began to feel oppressed by her sadness and the complete despair in her voice. I was relieved when it grew dark and we left the park to go our separate ways.

Two years later, in 2008, I came across the word 'bipolar' again. It was in a letter my daughter Daniella had written to her psychiatrist, telling him how grateful she was for the one-day workshop he had conducted on the subject. She wanted me to publish her letter in *The Shillong Times*, a paper I edit, but I didn't. I didn't have the courage. It still sits in my inbox. For years I had criticized people for being in denial about drug addiction, alcoholism, HIV & AIDS, and now I found I was equally culpable.

But this realization came later. That evening in 2006, I was relieved to let Yang go, taking her suffering out of my life, because I didn't want to accept that I had a Yang in my own home.

I WILL NEVER forget the morning Daniella was born. It was 26 April 1974. I was in my full term and the baby inside was beginning to push. The labour pains came with sharp, regular jabs. As soon as it was morning, I told my mother that I wanted to be taken to the

DANIELLA

local hospital. She and I took a taxi and landed in the Emergency. The doctor who assisted me during the birth was a happy-go-lucky sort. In the labour room of Nazareth Hospital, Shillong, while I was in agony, he whistled Elvis Presley's 'Wake up in the morning' and left the nurses to do what they could. After the umpteenth push, Daniella appeared, at 9.30 a.m. All that the doctor did was to repair my torn birth canal. His behaviour seemed all of a piece with the masculine indifference I had confronted at various stages of my life.

Daniella's father had no part to play in that hospital room. We Khasis don't believe in arranged marriages. Cohabitation—where man and woman live with each other like a 'married' couple, with all the attendant responsibilities—is part of our culture. But the man who fathered Daniella was not a Khasi and did not get this. He was not willing to take responsibility for the child he had fathered. He made that clear on the day I announced I was pregnant. Until then, I had assumed that we were in love and that his commitment to me would include the outcome of our love. It didn't. Well, I'd have to live with that. It didn't really matter as long as he gave the baby his name. It's important that we know who our parents are, even if they aren't married. But Daniella was already on to a bad start; her father wasn't going to acknowledge his role in her birth.

As I lay in the hospital with her downy head nuzzling my breast, I knew it wasn't going to be easy. Mary Jones, my firstborn—more friend than daughter, with only seventeen years separating us—was just three years old then. She was at a playschool in the neighbourhood. My mother looked after her through the day while I worked mornings as a teacher in a local English-medium school and gave private tuitions in the afternoons to supplement my salary. Thank God I had no siblings to support or look after or I would not have been able to graduate after Mary Jones was born. Then, too, I had loved well but not wisely. Then, too, my lover had ditched me when he found out I was pregnant. But at least he had given Mary his name.

Even so a family storm had burst around my head that first time. My mother, Mei, was in tears, my stepfather livid. At night I could hear angry exchanges between them about my future and the future of Mary Jones.

Stepfather: 'And who is going to look after this baby?'

Mei: 'If she agrees to go back to college I will go out and work and bring home some money. Delphi can look after the baby during the day.'

Delphina was my mother's sister who lived with us. Neither of these women said anything to me; perhaps they were afraid of what I would do.

Two months after Mary Jones was born, I went back to college, enrolled for History Honours and gave all attention to my studies. But I was lonely and miserable and started looking for companionship. That was when I met the man who would be Daniella's father. And once again, in the months before my BA final examination, I found myself pregnant.

Heavy with child, I wrote two examination papers. There was a gap of a fortnight before the next two. It was at this crucial juncture that Daniella was born. After four days in hospital, I went home and hit the books again. When Daniella was hungry, I breast-fed her. When she slept, I studied. I wrote the papers with painful, swollen breasts. Sometime into the third exam paper there was a

DANIELLA

shooting pain and milk began to drip from my nipples. My clothes were sodden. I looked around to see if anyone had noticed but thankfully all heads were down, everyone scribbling furiously. I dug a shawl out of my bag, wrapped up, completed my paper and rushed home in a taxi.

For the next two days, a fever raged through me. I could not study for the last paper. I relied on what I could remember and wrote what I could. Two months later, I graduated, scoring far higher than I had expected to; somehow, I had surmounted the odds I had imposed upon myself. I found a teaching job. I paid my way. As is the custom in Khasi society, I continued to live with my mother and stepfather.

Mary Jones and Daniella both studied at the school I was teaching in. The nuns were kind and gave me secondhand children's clothes that came from Italy and elsewhere and were meant to be distributed to the poor. We survived on my salary and this generous charity. But my kids felt the pinch. By an unspoken agreement, they did not ask about their fathers.

Some years later, I shifted both Mary Jones and Daniella to Loreto Convent. At the time Mary was in Class V and Daniella in Class II. The crème de la crème of society attended Loreto Convent and I was determined to work as hard as I had to in order to keep my girls at this school. My mother wouldn't have been able to afford the fees for me. Mary Jones sailed through high school with flying colours and got into medical college.

Meanwhile, the story of my romance with life had not stopped. I met another man who gave me two more daughters. One of them died at nine months. The other, Dorothea, is a fine young lady today. My final fling gave me a son. None of these liaisons lasted. I blame no one. My life is what it is. My choices were what they were.

Except for giving birth to my children, I was never really a mother. It was Mei who cared for them, brought them up, tutored them, dropped them to school and brought them back. Delphina, a widow with two sons, pitched in. Delphina virtually lived with us and my children saw in her a second grandmother to nurse their wounds and hurts when Mei or I censured them for their pranks or bad behaviour. She and Daniella shared a very special relationship. Everyone could see that my aunt showered all her affection on Daniella. Perhaps Daniella filled a need in her for a daughter. Delphina had lost a daughter in what doctors call a 'cot death'; the little thing had probably suffocated. My aunt lived with that guilt. This is conjecture, of course; it is difficult to say what draws one person to another. Delphina passed away in 2003 when a blood vessel burst in her brain. Daniella was twenty-nine years old but she was devastated. It was as if she had lost her anchor.

When she had finished school, barely eighteen, Daniella announced that she wanted to go to college in Kolkata.
'How are we going to afford that?' I asked her.
'I want to go,' she said stubbornly. 'All my friends are leaving Shillong for studies. I want to do English Honours.'
'I hardly earn enough to make ends meet. How will I pay for your hostel and travel?' I argued.
'Don't worry,' she said, 'I'll enroll in morning college and work during the day.'
'You're too young to work,' I said.
'I'm not.'
'Who will look after you there?'

DANIELLA

'Don't worry, Meipat,' she said, using the name the kids have for me, 'you've done your bit. Now I'm going to fend for myself.'

Finally, I gave in. I only made one condition: she should study as a regular student. I would take on more hours of tuition to earn extra money.

Daniella got into Loreto College, Kolkata, and started classes. I did not worry too much about her. I assumed she would sail through college as she had through school. She called home often and things seemed to be going well. 'I'm very happy here. English Honours is very interesting,' she said and giggled. That was Daniella's trademark. She giggled when she spoke. And when she laughed, her eyes shone with tears.

There was a moment of worry when she wrote asking details of her father. I told her his name, and that he was now someone important in the Arunachal Pradesh government, but I also explained that he had never shown any interest in meeting her. She did not mention it again. But then news arrived that she was going around with a boy whom she had known in Shillong and who had also moved to Kolkata to study, and I began to worry. I remembered my own mistakes; I did not want my daughters to struggle as I had done. I wrote Daniella a letter. (Those were the days of snail mail.) She wrote back admitting that she was seeing him but that I should not worry. She sounded mature and confident and I was relieved.

The relief was short-lived. Her first year exams had just started when I got a frantic call from her dear friend Karen.

'Aunty, I don't know what's happened to Daniella. She didn't go to write her exam today. She looks unwell,' Karen said.

'What happened? How can I reach her? Is there a telephone nearby?' I asked.

'No, we've taken her to hospital,' Karen said warily.

In my panic and worry I asked, 'Is she pregnant?'

'No, Aunty, I think she's depressed.'

'Depressed? What's that supposed to mean?' Now I was almost in tears. 'Who told you she is depressed?'

'Aunty, that's what the doctor said.'

I told Karen to book Daniella on a flight home immediately. She'll be all right when she gets back, I told myself. Delphina and I will get her on her feet again. She missed all of us, that's all. Depressed? What do these doctors know? We're Khasi women. We're strong.

But when Daniella came home I could not recognize my little darling. She looked frail and anaemic. Karen had told me that she had not been eating well but surely she could not have starved herself into this state?

'Are you pregnant? Did you have an abortion?' I asked her later that day.

She looked at me, shocked. 'I did nothing like that, Meipat. I just didn't feel like studying English Honours.'

'Why did you want to go to Kolkata then?' I said, making little effort to keep the anger out of my voice.

'It didn't work out,' she said, offering no explanation. 'If you can support me with four thousand rupees, I'll go back to Kolkata and join the Birla Institute of Liberal Arts. I want to do their advertising management course. I promise I won't let you down.'

I agreed. Daniella left Shillong four weeks later when she was better and joined the institute. Unknown to me, she also took up a part-time job at a computer firm. She completed her course and armed with that certificate, found herself a job at Hewlett-Packard.

DANIELLA

She enrolled at South City College; in due course, she graduated with English Honours.

Meanwhile my youngest child, Jude, enrolled at Scottish Church College, Kolkata. By then I had shifted to H. Elias Memorial School, a missionary school, and was earning a decent salary. Mary Jones had completed her medical degree and was posted to a rural hospital in Meghalaya. Jude did not have to worry about a part-time job, I sent him enough money every month. He stayed in the same hostel as Daniella. I found this reassuring. I forgot that Jude was too young to notice any changes in Daniella's mental or physical condition.

In June 2000, Karen called again. Daniella had gone to spend the weekend with her and had taken ill. She had been admitted to hospital.

'What do the doctors say?' I asked Karen. 'Can I speak to her?'

'There's a phone next to her bed. I'll connect you,' Karen said.

Daniella's voice sounded weak, teary. In a faint voice she said it was malarial jaundice.

'I'm coming down tomorrow, baby,' I told her, my heart breaking. 'Don't worry, just tell the doctors to do their best…I'm coming.'

I broke down. Mary Jones took charge immediately. 'Meipat, I'll go,' she said. 'I'm a doctor; I'm better placed to look after her.'

Mary Jones had married a social anthropologist, Morrison, in 1998 and moved to Ahmedabad with him, but she was with us in Shillong at that time, recuperating after a miscarriage. She showed greater strength and presence of mind than me. She flew to Kolkata and called me from Salt Lake City the next day. Daniella was delirious, she said, and in the intensive care unit. 'It's serious, but the doctors are doing their best. Just pray that she recovers,' she said.

Daniella was shifted to a multi-specialty hospital. Her lungs had almost collapsed due to fluid retention. She was on oxygen. Medicines were pumped into her fragile system intravenously. I was part of a Christian fellowship group and we stormed heaven round the clock. 'God, help her to recover,' I prayed, tears flowing freely. 'We have not seen each other for a while. I plead with you, Giver of Life. Heal Daniella and give me time to be with her.'

God heard my prayers. Daniella recovered miraculously. She had begun to eat solid food and Mary Jones reported that they would return home in about a week's time after she was released from hospital.

It was with trepidation that I went to receive my two girls at the airport. One frail and weak, the other a guardian angel who had taken my place and mothered her little sister. I held back my tears. 'I have to be strong,' I told myself. 'After all, the worst is over.'

But I spoke too soon.

Daniella recovered physically and began looking for a job. Mary Jones and I noticed that she had become loud and garrulous, but we did not take this change seriously. We thought she had developed some city smarts and that it was a passing phase. Besides, she was not the only ill person in the family. Diabetes had claimed my stepfather in February 1999, two years before Daniella's return to Shillong. Mei, too, had been keeping indifferent health for a while. In March 2000, I was told by the medical specialist treating her that it was chronic renal failure. She had to be taken to hospital every now and again for dialysis.

It was a time of change, constant change, for all of us. I was

DANIELLA

freelancing as a columnist and independent researcher, travelling extensively within the country and outside. And so when Daniella recovered and chose to stay in Shillong, finding a job in the university, we all heaved a sigh of relief and got on with all the other things that were preoccupying us.

Meanwhile Mei's health deteriorated rapidly. She passed away in July 2001. Mary Jones had conceived again. She was in her third month and was advised against travelling. She could not come home for Mei's funeral. Daniella took charge and showed a maturity beyond her years.

But perhaps the family tragedies and general instability were taking their toll. She behaved abnormally at times. One day she announced that she was leaving home to stay in a rented place. I didn't take her seriously, but when I came home from work that evening, I was told that she had taken her luggage and left. I was livid. I refused to go looking for her or to call her friends.

She returned the next morning, and I was shocked to see her. Daniella was the beauty in the family. She was petite, and looked good in any kind of outfit, particularly the Western clothes that she favoured. She experimented all the time with different hairstyles, from crop to bob-cut, taking great care to look well groomed. But now she stood before me looking almost spectral. Her clothes were rumpled. There were dark circles under her eyes. Her lips were dark and dry. She seemed to have poured a full bottle of oil on her head.

It was the first clear sign to me that something was seriously wrong. Fear gripped me and for the first time I felt I had lost my child. She went to her bedroom quietly. It took me a while to recover, then I took a deep breath, willed myself to be calm and went to her room.

'Why did you do this? Did anyone here tell you to leave? Are you angry about something?'

She lay on her bed and looked at me blankly.

'Come on. Talk to me. You can't just come and go as you please,' I said.

She said nothing. I could feel my resolve to be calm wither away. And then my restraint snapped and I was off. Even as I shouted at her I knew that I was handling it all wrong. I look back now and wonder who needed counselling more, the daughter lying quietly on the bed or the mother ranting and raving beside it?

And yet there were still days when she would be really funny and make us laugh. Those were moments we all treasured because we were unsure when the next bout of anger and silence would shatter our little world. Like all mothers who fear to pronounce the worst about their kids, I remained in denial about the severity of Daniella's condition. Her siblings, too, would laugh off her unpredictable behaviour and put it down to the malarial jaundice.

Then came Delphine's death, which affected Daniella badly and she was withdrawn and listless for a long time. But the next year, in 2004, we were all hopeful again. Daniella had become friendly with a wonderful, quiet young man, Abel. They seemed to be very much in love. I was relieved. I thought he would be good for her; he was so patient and kind.

This seemed to help, but not for long. Her mood swings only seemed to get worse. That year, she said she wanted to get to know her father. She had looked him up on the internet and made contact with him through a mutual friend. She knew, of course, that he had been a minister in the Arunachal Pradesh government, so it was easy to track him. She now knew that he had married sometime after we parted and had two children. I had learned from someone that he was suffering from severe depression; if she had also discovered this, she did not tell me.

One day she announced she was going to Itanagar to meet him. She said she wanted to meet his children too.

I tried to dissuade her. 'Why Daniella? Why not put all this behind you? After all, you never knew him. How does it matter?'

She looked at me with something like disdain and said, 'Who are you to stop me? I have the right to know my father.'

I backed off. She left.

I lived in a state of dread until she called me from Itanagar, and then I was full of questions.

'How are things? How is your father, is he accepting you? And your half-sister and -brother? What about your father's wife?'

Finally, I asked the most difficult question. 'How is your father keeping? Is he in good health?'

'Everything is fine. Everyone here is very happy to see me,' she said. 'There are uncles and cousins and relatives and they have all come to see me. Only my father's wife does not seem happy.'

'Then why not come back now? You've met your father. Maybe you can invite him here.' I was petrified that they might ill-treat her or that she might decide to stay. I called her every day. My message was pretty much the same: 'Daniella, please come back. We miss you so much.'

She returned after a week. But something terrible had happened. She went for a bath and when she came out she had cut off her hair, as if in anger. No, cut is not the right word. She had hacked her hair off, she had wanted to wound herself.

'What happened, Daniella?' I asked, wounded myself. 'Why are you so angry? Did anyone hurt you in Itanagar?'

She looked at me as if I were a complete stranger. I could only pray and weep. Later that day I spoke to Mary Jones and asked her if I should take Daniella to a psychiatrist. She told me to do so immediately. The doctor listened patiently and then asked me to go out of the room. He sat with Daniella for about forty minutes and asked her to come back after a week. Later, over the telephone, he told me her mental state was 'fragile'.

I was confused and helpless. I did not know how to talk to her. I was afraid to even look at her. She was becoming unpredictable. At work she began to have frequent run-ins with her seniors. Most days she would say she was not feeling well and stay in her room. Her future worried me. At one point she told me, 'Uff, I hate that man! He's corrupt and shameless. Today he told me to fudge the accounts. I refused and he got angry. I don't know if I'm going to stick around in that place for too long.'

'Daniella, all of us live in an imperfect world,' I told her. 'If someone asks you to do the wrong thing, refuse gently. You have to learn to live in the real world.' But she finally did give up that job and became the communications consultant for a government-funded NGO.

Sometime later, someone from her new office called me to ask if everything was all right with Daniella. 'What do you mean, all right? Of course she is all right,' I said. I didn't want to jeopardize Daniella's future; I did what I had to so that she would keep her job. I denied to the world, to her and to myself that she needed help.

And so I failed her again. I paved the road to a hell of guilt with my good intentions.

DANIELLA

In January 2006, I went to the US for a year on a sabbatical of sorts, to write a book. I tried to work but I missed home and my children. I would call home almost every day. I spent the thousand-dollar-a-month stipend on phone calls. Daniella wrote emails to me regularly and I kept reassuring myself that she was well: she *had* to be well; she was writing about what was happening in Shillong, she was telling me about herself. But I could not shake off the guilt. I felt I was shirking my duties as a mother. In April 2006 I returned home without having written a single sentence of my book. I had agreed to stay there for a year, but I returned in three months. The US was a good place for research but my heart was not it. Besides, Daniella was repeatedly telling me that she and Abel were keen to get engaged and that they wanted me around.

When I returned, I saw that Daniella had changed even more. She would suddenly burst forth into speech, a dam split open as if under pressure. At other times, she would drift into silence. We had normal spells too, when she would talk excitedly about a film, or tell me about a picnic, her words coherent and logical, her emotions in sync with the moment, and I chose to focus on that Daniella. Underneath, I was worried about her, but I still did not understand just how serious things were. Or maybe I did not want to. Depression was normal, it was a phase. It would go away, it always did.

Through this period, I think it was only Abel who was her anchor. Shortly afterwards, Abel invited our family to his home to announce his intentions before his parents. We had lunch and exchanged pleasantries. Abel's parents seemed simple and kind. We set the date of the marriage: 20th November 2007.

Daniella was on medication now but she hated the pills and I suspect that she did not take the anti-depressants regularly. Overall, though, she seemed happy and in turn, we were happy. But then she'd suddenly have a bout of tears or a fit of shouting again and we would be back on our emotional roller-coaster.

Abel and Daniella had been very close friends ever since she returned from Kolkata in 2000. He was kind and patient, soft spoken and a man of few words. He and I would discuss Daniella's condition in confidence.

'Abel, I really don't know how to deal with her. I don't even know what she is suffering from. Do you think you can handle this relationship?' I asked him.

'Aunty, all she needs is patient listening. I know she has her moods, but I also know she is the one for me,' gentle Abel replied, almost as if he was talking to himself.

I never asked his age—it was not considered appropriate to do so—but I suspected he was a couple of years junior to Daniella. He showed a maturity beyond his years in dealing with his dilemma.

November 2007 came and we got ready with the wedding arrangements. We are Roman Catholics; Abel, a Baptist. After much hemming and hawing by the pastors of his church, we agreed on a mixed marriage in the Catholic church. Daniella looked glorious in her wedding gown. Abel, too, looked grand. Normally, in a Khasi family, the groom comes to the bride's home and stays there until such time they find a separate establishment. But Daniella and Abel did something that hurt me. They decided to stay in his home on the wedding night and thereafter. I did not express my hurt for fear that it would trigger a backlash.

Abel and Daniella seemed to have slid comfortably into their marriage and appeared happy. I called her every day to ask if all

DANIELLA

was well. Daniella had no complaints. She kept a good home and outwardly it was difficult to guess that she was fighting a battle inside. Four months after the marriage they shifted to their own place—a rented accommodation not very far from Abel's home. Friends and family were invited in batches for lunch or dinner. I was always wary, always watchful. I expected something to go wrong anytime.

Now that I look back at my relationship with Daniella, I realize how uneasy it was, how difficult it was for the two of us to have an intimate, even a proper conversation. She seemed to believe that I had high standards that she could not live up to. She would tell her colleagues with great pride about my work and achievements, but perhaps this also contributed to the feeling that she was not good enough.

But these are only conjectures, the wild guesses you make when you don't understand.

Daniella told Mary Jones that she wanted to conceive. Mary Jones took her to a gynaecologist. Daniella was told that her thyroid was not functioning well and that she had to take medicines. She hated medicines, we had to remind her all the time to take the anti-depressants regularly. And now she had other medicines to swallow.

Late in August 2008, Daniella wanted to visit Dimapur, Nagaland. Her mother-in-law was a Naga while her father-in-law was a Khasi. 'Let's go in December when you have Christmas holidays,' her mother-in-law said. 'No, I want to go next week,' Daniella insisted. Her mother-in-law gave in and they all drove to Dimapur. After spending a week there planting trees and flowers and visiting relatives, they all returned to Shillong. Daniella came home with lots of gifts. She looked happy.

SATURDAY, 13 SEPTEMBER 2008. I was at work, putting *The Shillong Times* to bed. Jude called.

'Mummy, please come to Daniella's home. She's not well.'

'What's wrong with her?'

'Please, just come.'

'Why not take her to the hospital?' I shouted, my anxiety out in the open.

'Mummy, just come here. Do you want us to pick you up?'

I called a taxi and rushed to Daniella's home. I think I knew already. I knew with a sick feeling in the pit of my stomach. But when I got there and saw her, lying dead in her bedroom, pills all over the floor, I could not believe it. My Daniella?

She had been alone at home. Abel was away at work. Daniella, he said, was not been keeping too well but she had told him to go, she would be okay. The mobile phone was next to her bed but she had not called anyone. Not Abel, not her sister or brother. Not her mother.

Just days before, she had been so happy, full of details about the journey to Dimapur.

'How did this happen?' I asked Abel.

He broke down and could not answer me. I realize he could have asked each one of us the same question: How did this happen? Because a suicide is like that; it becomes a series of unanswered questions. Everyone who loved that person asks: What did I do? What did I not do? Did I not hear the cry for help? How could I not see this coming? How could she do this? Why did she not feel close enough to call me in her moment of despair? Did she think I would not understand? Did she think I would not give her permission to leave this world?

DANIELLA

How can a child born of one's womb be so estranged?

By then, several friends had come to know. I will never forget R.G. Lyngdoh, the former home minister of Meghalaya, who came up to me and said, 'Kong, this is not the time for us to find fault or blame anyone. Please.'

Okay, so even if I could do this, if I could free myself of guilt and blame, if I could release all the others who knew her, what then? Should I just accept Daniella's death as natural? How did she die? Was she so troubled by her condition that she found it too hard to continue? Why didn't she call?

I ask these questions over and over again even today as I sit and write this and look at her lovely photo…all smiles, yet sad. Always. Even the narratives she brought home from her office were about some underdog struggling for her rights. Perhaps she identified with them because they too were struggling to cope with life.

I miss her every day. I ask the same question every day and now it has boiled down to a single syllable: why? It's a powerful question and sometimes I direct it at myself, sometimes at God, sometimes at Nature.

But no answers come.

It is eight years since Daniella left us, yet none of us in the family dare discuss her mental state. I don't know if we are doing the right thing. It has not been easy to write this, and I know I have still not looked truth in the eye. Mary Jones, Jude and Dorothea, Daniella's younger sister with whom she had the least interface, only talk about the good times, about the funny things she said and did that made us laugh. We are all coping in our own ways and I wonder sometimes if we all need to see a therapist.

And what about Abel? And his mother, who loved Daniella like her own daughter in the short time that she stayed with them? In the first few months after her death, Abel would visit her grave and sit there to console himself; light a candle and perhaps shed tears. Two months after her death he put up a unique tombstone, a piece of granite. He got it cut in the shape of Moses's tablet and placed it at the head of the grave. A sculpture of an angel with folded hands lies at her feet. Daniella's grave has become a convergence point for the family and a place where we find solace when things are on top of us.

With time memories fade and I regret to say this but my interface with Abel's family has dwindled to occasional visits and a casual conversation over the telephone. Those left behind, the living, must find ways to carry on.

I speak to Daniella all the time, almost as if she is still around. That is how I carry on, how I cope with the survivor's guilt. I believe my Daniella's spirit continues to hover around the house. When I am low and miserable I look at her smiling picture and a sense of peace envelops me. She is next to me, hugging me in her arms. I can hear her say, 'Meipat, take it easy, no stress. Take your medicines on time. And remember to drink some fruit juice or eat some nuts before you step out for a walk.'

THE MAN UNDER THE STAIRCASE

Sharmila Joshi

THEY FOUND VINAY by the side of the street on a misty winter morning. A man on a bicycle saw him from across the street. Vinay looked like he was resting after a long night, stopping by in the pale shade of the neem in the early sunlight. His head was on the pavement, his left cheek pressed on the asphalt. The cyclist crossed the street and joined a gathering knot of people. Vinay was still, unobtrusive in death as he had been when alive, except for the acrid smell of alcohol rising thinly into the cold morning air.

That's Judge-bhau's brother, someone said. In Nagpur's neighbourhoods in the early 1970s, people knew each other. In Ramdaspeth, they all knew Vinay, though for years he had rarely ventured out before dark, and then too only in pursuit of a quarter bottle. The bicyclist who recognized Vinay offered to tell the Judge that his brother was lying dead, down the street. He cycled off to the bungalow with the first Impala in town, a white car with red flanks resting in the driveway like a misguided aeroplane.

Vinay had lived in this house on East High Court Road almost all his life, the last years in a space far less flamboyant than the car. His abode was the alcove under the staircase that led up to the terrace, just beyond the kitchen at the back of the house. At night he slept on a worn durrie, during the day he sat on the same durrie. When the cold winter crept into Nagpur, my mother would surreptitiously give Vinay old blankets.

Every year, she would ask my father, the Judge, to allow Vinay to live in the house, in one of the unused rooms at the back. When my father would once again fulminate that he did not want the drunk inside the house, she would ask if Vinay could at least sleep in the garage, which was too small for the big new car.

The Judge's response never wavered: he was, he said, being kind to his useless brother by allowing him to stay below the staircase. He did not want Vinay to wander about drunk in Ramdaspeth. What would people say if they saw the honourable Judge's brother sleeping on the street? They would say that the Judge has no mercy. Keeping Vinay tucked away in the stairwell, the Judge hoped, would erase from people's memory, and his own, all thought about the derelict.

And Vinay seemed to be content with his patch of home, at least it looked like that to me. He was quiet most of the time. On some days he talked sparingly with the cook who handed him a plate of food, or he exchanged a few brief words with the gardener when he used the water tap at the end of the backyard. Most of the time during the day, he slept. Sometimes, he sketched.

Before dusk overtook the day and his soul and he left the dark stairs to wander through the darkening neighbourhoods of Nagpur looking for someone who would give the Judge's brother country liquor on credit—during those few fleetingly lucid hours, Vinay sketched. His thin fingers filled up unused pages of my old school notebooks, which he salvaged every few months from the raddiwala. I kept the stubs of my old pencils for him and would gladly have

THE MAN UNDER THE STAIRCASE

given him all my notebooks, but was too frightened of my father's disapproval.

Vinay would sit on the old dark-blue durrie, back resting against the wall, in his one pair of faded grey trousers and white shirt, a notebook resting on his knees. The fine lines that slowly spread across the page reflected the delicate planes of his face. He drew from memory, of a life long lost—images of his school, corners of his childhood home, the faces of people he had met, the landscapes of Nagpur. And sometimes what he drew was from another, internal world—bursts of agonized scrawls and clusters of brooding shades. A dusty heap of old notebooks had grown under the stairs. This heap was Vinay's second most treasured possession.

Sometimes, when I was running up the stairs to the terrace, Vinay would wordlessly show me a sketch he was working on. I would glance at it and run along, always a little afraid, at the age of eight, of the shadows and smells of Vinay's musty dwelling lit by the lone 25-watt bulb. Always desperately hoping that the afternoon would not give way to a night when my father would go out to the stairs in a rage at Vinay, who sometimes staggered back close to dawn. Always dreading that endless moment when the beating began. My father was a big man, and Vinay was frail. He took the blows silently.

Vinay's most prized possession was a battered old guitar, which rested in the groove under the lowest step of the staircase. On days when the shadows cleared a little inside his head, Vinay would pick up the guitar and start playing. A web of soft music would then drift away towards the terrace. Sweet tunes and heartbreaking strains would echo through the shadows. I looked forward eagerly to those evenings.

Vinay loved music. He would silently signal to me, with a shy half-smile, when the hallway door was open, to play an LP for him on our radiogram. I was not supposed to touch the oversized old record player, but when my father was away at the court, my mother did not say anything if I took off the cloth cover and picked out a record I knew Vinay liked—jazz greats, old Hindi film melodies, at times a bhajan or Bhimsen Joshi. Sometimes, he and I listened to Akashwani together, Vinay sitting outside the door on the floor, while I sat on the huge red sofa in the hall, my feet dangling. Every now and then, the radio programmes would be interrupted for news about the latest attacks and counter-attacks. It was 1971 and we were at war.

The more immediate battles that erupted in our world were between Vinay and Ashu. Ashu was our neighbour, my best friend Anju's much older sister, then in her twenties. At the age of eight, after a prolonged trip with her family to Bombay, she had become severely mentally disturbed. I don't know what had happened to Ashu that destroyed her universe. She spent the day, every day, sitting on the kitchen floor of their house, always in a white petticoat and blue blouse, hitting her forehead and repeating her name, over and over again. She swayed with every slap.

Her left eye had become opaque because of this incessant infliction. Every effort to make her stop had failed. She would stop only if someone physically restrained her or if she was sedated, but as soon as she was awake and unrestrained, she would start again. When the torment of Ashu's demons became unbearable, she would start screaming, incoherent piercing sounds that echoed through the walls. I was terrified of these sounds—and of Ashu.

We could hear her screams over the compound wall and across

THE MAN UNDER THE STAIRCASE

the short distance that separated the two houses. If she started shouting on an evening when Vinay was at the staircase and not wandering about on the streets, and if he was already drunk (with a quarter bottle clumsily hidden from my father beneath a blanket), he would shout back at Ashu. Why are you shrieking, he would ask her, and order her to shut up and go to sleep.

The two would then have a roaring dialogue of garbled words that went back and forth from our house to theirs, a thread of communication slowly building between two lonely people adrift in a bewildering world. On these evenings, if my father was at home, he would become furious with the shouting and he would go out of the hall door to strike Vinay.

Vinay emerged from these brutalities seemingly unscathed. The next afternoon, when he woke up, he would open his notebook and start sketching. Or by early evening, he would pick up his guitar and strum a tune he had heard when I played a record for him. If Vinay's spirit had not been so steeped in alcohol, he might have become an accomplished musician.

He was sixteen when he gave up trying to complete high school. He had played guitar in a school band and he dropped out to join Nagpur's most popular orchestra. With the first few payments he bought the guitar. The orchestra played at various official events and at the wedding receptions of Nagpur's wealthy and well-connected, such as the residents of our neighbourhood.

My grandmother had disapproved of Vinay's choice of work and his love of music. Her older son, my father, was already a lawyer. How could her younger son play in a band? But Vinay would not do anything else. My mother told me that in those days he talked to her of his dreams of recording an album, of trying his luck as a music director in then faraway Bombay's glittering film world.

No one knows when and how Vinay started drinking, or when he progressed from an occasional drink to regular drinking to heavy drinking, and then to near-constant intoxication. My mother remembers giving him money to buy balloons and Ravalgaon toffees for my first birthday. A small party was being organized in our front garden. Vinay returned without the balloons and toffees, smelling of rum. This was the first time my family realized that Vinay, only twenty then, had already been drinking regularly for a few years.

Vinay played the guitar with the orchestra until he was twenty-six. Even then, he rarely talked to anyone. No one knew what was happening within this quiet young man. My father was busy at the Nagpur High Court. My grandfather was long gone and my grandmother doted on my father. She scolded Vinay every night when he came home, while giving him a plate of cold dal and rice, but she made no real attempt to talk to her younger son. Vinay's dreams and demons, his hopes and anxieties, remained concealed.

One day, when Vinay returned to the house at Ramdaspeth after a tour with the orchestra of the towns of eastern Maharashtra, he found a padlock on the door to his room. That was the year my grandmother died. With her gone, my father no longer felt compelled to keep his brother in the house. Vinay's handful of clothes and things had been shifted to the stairwell.

With this, Vinay moved out of the house and moved further within himself. With the shrinking of the physical space he occupied at the house, his external world also became smaller. His orchestra assignments became fewer. If he was too drunk, he began

THE MAN UNDER THE STAIRCASE

to skip even the sporadic work that came his way. Eventually, the assignments stopped altogether and Vinay confined himself to his spot under the stairway, becoming more reticent, more melancholy.

When I was nine, my mother and I moved to Bombay. My mother was no longer able or willing to handle the abuse and the violence my father routinely inflicted on her. For the first few months in Bombay, I missed Nagpur desperately. I missed Ramdaspeth, my old school, our dog, I missed my friend Anju. And I missed my uncle Vinay.

My father remarried within a year of our moving out. Vinay was asked to vacate the patch of stairway shelter he had occupied for four years. He left wordlessly and wandered about for days, sleeping on the streets, begging at dhabas. He eventually moved into a slum colony near the Sadar Bazaar area. By then my father had cut off all contact with his younger brother.

My friend Anju wrote letters to me about our school, our friends, and the other minutiae of our childhood in Nagpur. A few months after we moved to Bombay, she wrote in a blue inland letter that her sister Ashu had died of a cerebral haemorrhage. A few times she wrote that she or another friend had seen my uncle—a dreaded but fascinating figure to all the children on our street—when they were on their way to school. Once she saw him sitting on the pavement on East High Court Road, near our house. In letters that Anju's mother wrote to my mother, she mentioned that they had seen Vinay in Sadar Bazaar begging silently for food and money, or sprawled near the country liquor shop at the edge of the market.

Vinay died within a year of losing his stairway home. He had just turned thirty. His liver could not handle the alcohol. And his heart, I believe, had a hole which got bigger with time as he struggled with the sorrow of dealing with a world that he could not fit into. A small crowd gathered around Vinay lying cold on the wide empty street that winter morning in Ramdaspeth. The cyclist came to our house, rang the doorbell, and told my father.

A few months after Vinay died, my father, overcome with a fleeting grief, came to visit us in Mumbai. He cried and raged against his brother who, he said, had damaged the family's reputation. I was nearly ten then. I went to the window that faced the sea, and cried for my gentle uncle, always lost and now gone forever.

After my father left, my mother searched for photographs of Vinay to put in a frame. She could not find any. The only photograph of him that I recall remained in an album in Nagpur. In this photo, Vinay is looking intensely, unsmiling, at the camera, a lock of fashionably oiled hair falling across his forehead. He is on his way to buy balloons for my first birthday party. Years later, when I asked my father for the photograph, he said it was damaged. Its edges had curled up and the image had bleached out.

I still have a sketch that Vinay gave me as a gift on my eighth birthday. On this frayed page of my old notebook, dark neem trees cast merciful shadows across the street.

ABHIMANYU, OUR SON

Madhusudan Srinivas

THIS IS A small story, a look-in through a tiny window at our life. It's about our son Abhimanyu, his autism, and about us. But we have to tell you that it isn't the full story, there's a lot more to it.

Abhimanyu is 23, about five feet eleven inches tall. He lives with us, his parents, both journalists, in New Delhi. He is taller than both of us, towering over us like a 'gentle giant', as one of his teachers calls him.

I wouldn't be exaggerating if I say everyone loves him. He is, and has always been, a cheery, happy fellow, with a grin plastered across his face. He smiles thus, whatever the circumstances—it could be an inability to understand what's going on around him, an inability to speak full sentences, or extreme sensory distress which makes him clap or screech loudly in public.

It is this smile that has kept us going all these years.

It kept us going in the face of extreme distress, on his part, when he would cry for hours together, or have a tantrum, while we tried desperately to understand what was going on with him—the crying was so intense sometimes that the only way to soothe him was to pull him into the car and drive for hours around the city.

And it kept me going in the face of crippling embarrassment when I would take him out and he would 'behave oddly': how many children of ten or eleven do you see flapping their arms and screeching and rocking? How many young adults do you see with a wet patch on their crotch?

We knew that this wetting was not due to not being 'toilet trained'. We knew, by then, that his seizures, which began when he was around eleven, could be the cause: they could be overt or subliminal, under the surface, and we would have to be on our guard all the time. But how do you explain to people who do not know about autism, or have met him for the first time, that he could wet the sofa or their bed without warning? On the whole, though, people have been very understanding, and we count our blessings.

The wetting still happens. The bewilderment we sometimes see on his face is a constant feature: so many times we think he's trying to tell us something but doesn't have the tools to. We end up surmising, sometimes right, sometimes wrong. I have to be especially alert because I take him out with me as often as I can; I have always believed that my son needs to be out and about, in public transport, in movie halls, even if he spills popcorn and is not really interested in what's going on on the screen.

In our journey with him, we have been accompanied by so many people who also know him well enough to figure out what he may want (there are times he will say a few words out loud, because he does have limited speech for his wants; at other times a sharp clap is a communicating strategy). We have our two 'didis', who live with us; our neighbours, who make it a point always to greet him; our numerous friends and our family, all of whom I try to keep informed about Abhi's everyday life. We have a great support system, and I would like to think that I have been instrumental in creating it, speaking to as many people as I can, making bridges online and off: journalism and autism, for me, have gone hand in hand.

Most often we get by. We get busy with work and friends. And Abhi spends his time at 'school' (the Ashish Centre for young people with autism, where he is learning basic life skills from loving, caring people, therapists and teachers who are madly fond of him).

He wins everyone over with his gigantic smile. It makes us forget. But then comes that occasional seizure which stops us in our tracks, which gets us started on the long, weary checklist all over again: is his medication at the right level, does it need to be re-jigged, do we need to switch doctors? It makes me wake up with a start even before the daily alarm goes off at four in the morning in my bedroom just above Abhimanyu's in our split-level home, my first thought being: 'Have I the energy to go down and check if he's okay?'

That reluctance could be because the day gone by was a tough one, and because I'm always sleep deprived. Or because we've had a rare late evening, snatching a few hours away from our darling child. On such nights I could come back wondering whether my boy is asleep. Or whether he's had a seizure that we haven't managed to catch, which sometimes leads to loss of bladder control, then and afterwards.

And yet the life we lead, bringing up our child, a young man who hasn't spoken a clear full sentence to us in all the years since he was born, and then diagnosed with autism at nearly three—our precarious life together—is also supremely happy. I would not trade it for any other even if he is not and will never be like other children; in some ways, he will always be a child.

Growing up, he's said 'Rajma dey do', he's said 'Swimming jaana', he's said a myriad other things, mumbled in his unintelligible-to-the-world-but-clear-to-us monotone. He didn't listen to Justin Bieber or One Direction at age thirteen. He hasn't demanded to be taken to a concert in the Philippines by a band of the moment or a raging sex symbol.

But he's young too, showing us flashes of his growing will. And he has his range of music to go to, his fallback options ranging from A.R. Rahman to the Gundecha brothers to the latest Bollywood ditty. Music is his life, as it is ours. It was always so, now it is so more than ever…

So what am I trying to tell you? What am I trying to say, writing these words to share with you what lies beyond the six degrees of separation in the lives of people like us, Abhimanyu's parents, and many other parents like us who have been given a diagnosis of differentness? I'm saying: Most of our children haven't demanded anything of us, ever. It's we who end up demanding a hell of a lot of them in our endeavour to meet society's norms. To make the differently abled as non-different and as indistinguishable as we can. To gain 'acceptance'—in the family, the home, the housing society, the mohalla, the street, the main road, the mall, the multiplex, the metro line, the market, the world at large.

I'm saying: We live; a kind of life, like all the other lives that are lived. And this world is as much Abhimanyu's as anybody else's.

That's as much of a window as we could open right now. The entire house tour some other day.

ROGER, OVER AND OUT

Lalita Iyer

'I CAN CARRY you over,' he said.

It was her earliest and most vivid memory of Roger. It was the kind of afternoon that pretends to be an evening and Kavya was staring at a puddle that seemed to have emerged out of nowhere, right in front of her. She was trekking through the spice villages of Kumily, near Thekkady, and Roger Nyström was her tour guide that afternoon. The puddle was too wide for her to jump across and just shallow enough to soak her shoes and leave them clammy for the rest of the evening. She wondered if it was too early to be out walking in the wilderness with him, considering they had met just yesterday, but she brushed the thought aside. She was on holiday; adventure was part of the deal. But in her oversized dungarees (which folded over her heels and dragged, fashionably) and her Woodland shoes which didn't live up to their promise of being water repellent, she was clearly not ready for the hinterlands of Periyar. She was still wondering how to navigate the puddle, when the voice spoke again.

'I can carry you over. If that's okay with you.'

'Ummm, okay then.'

And that's where it all started.

Kavya was on an impulse holiday. It was one of those things she did often these days. It had become important for her to listen to her gut. It had made her abandon a career in biochemistry after a Master's degree because, suddenly, her heart was not in it. It was her unruly gut that made her join an advertising agency as a copywriter, her demanding gut that made her walk out of her parents' home at twenty-four and move into a hostel, because she wanted to do life on her own terms and didn't want to explain why she was late and who she was with. The same recalcitrant gut made her, five years into advertising, realize it was not her calling, and quit.

Without a Plan B.

Travelling after quitting had become a routine. She had to do it before things got too real and she felt the need to find a job again. The only difference this time was that her gut wanted her to travel alone. 'I want to do Kerala,' she thought. Cochin, because a city that ran on waterways always intrigued her. Trichur, the hometown of her friend, Radhika. Alleppey, because you cannot not do backwaters, plus she loved water hyacinths. Definitely Thekkady. The images of Rekha and Naseeruddin Shah honeymooning amid half-immersed tree stumps in the movie *Ijaazat* on the banks the quiet Periyar Lake were fresh in her mind, although at that time she didn't see the ecological disaster embedded in the beauty and lyricism of Gulzar's shot-taking. Her itinerary allowed four days in Thekkady, skirting the Periyar sanctuary.

The bit about 'woman travelling alone' didn't seem to get in her way as much as she thought, and she was grateful for that. In her spirit of 'let me do some wildlife', she had checked into the Periyar Forest Guest House on the banks of the lake and discovered, to

ROGER, OVER AND OUT

her horror on night one, that it was home to a bunch of riotous, drum-banging, antakshari-playing tourists. The activist in her raised an alarm at midnight, asking to speak to the forest officer about possible damage to the animals in the sanctuary. The realist checked out the next morning and moved to Ambady Guest House outside the sanctuary.

So much for *Ijaazat*. But then, that was Rekha.

Day two found her wandering into Coffee Inn, en route to the Periyar Wildlife Sanctuary on Thekkady Road. It was a quiet, quaint sort of place, overlooking a spice garden, and played some kind of Buddha bar music. On the menu were smoothies, peanut butter jelly sandwiches, different types of tea, fresh fruit platters and pancakes, the kind of comfort food that eased the effects of the excesses of the Periyar Guest House with its ostentatious buffet. Plus any place where the waiters weren't eager to thrust their menus at you and get chatty with 'Where are you from?' was welcome to Kavya. She settled down with a lemon tea and PBJ sandwich and looked wistfully at the garden outside.

She spent the next half hour daydreaming, something she hadn't done in a while. She could be doing this for life, she thought. Running a cafe in a faraway place, maybe a library so she could meet book lovers, maybe selling knick-knacks and stuff. On her way out, she stared long and hard at the postcards on the display board, reading notes from all over the world to Shaju, the proprietor. This is the kind of love that could come my way, she thought. Some postcards were in French and German, and she didn't really know what they said, but the shape of the words interested her anyway.

'That's quite a few languages you read,' said a voice. It came from a kind face, with blue eyes, a two-day stubble, cargo pants and a denim shirt. The body attached to the face was tall, and stooping, like someone used to constantly bending to talk to people.

'I don't, actually. I was just trying to feel the words,' she said.

'That's a good way to become friends with them,' said Mr Blue Eyes.

She liked him.

'Roger,' he said.

'Kavya,' she replied and they shook hands. Nice hands, she said to herself, kind hands.

'See you around then,' he said and walked off.

It was time for her to unpack in her new home, Hotel Ambady. She liked doing up her room even if she was just passing through. So that's what she did for the rest of the evening, sorting her clothes, shoes, hanging them up, lighting an agarbatti, settling in, making it home.

By the next day, Coffee Inn was home too. She came there for breakfast, lunch and dinner and everything in between. She also hoped that she would run into Roger again. This was in the time before mobile phones, before Facebook, before WhatsApp. Only the geeks did email and you heard of it as a tremor from another world, that First World which was always in a rush. In those days, you only had fate to rely on.

Shaju had turned from indifferent to chatty, now that it was established that she was a regular. He had a carefully cultivated breezy air about him. It was like he was seeking information, but not processing it.

'Where are you staying?' he asked.

'I was at Periyar Guest House. But I just moved to Ambady,' she said, hoping to be redeemed.

Kavya had been marked. At Rs 1,500 a night, Periyar Guest House was home to the rich and the lazy. People who lived there ordered room service, booked cars and hired guides for plantation tours. Hotel Ambady was the gauche cousin; she had oil in her hair and a smile on her face.

'Oh, you are a rich girl, ah?'

'No, it's only seven hundred a night,' she said.

'We have huts at Coffee Inn for three hundred per night. But it's not for posh people like you.'

'I'm not posh. Can I see them?'

'Just go this way from the garden, and it's on the backside. You might see Roja,' he added.

Adventure again. It might be nice to live in a hut, although she just had two more days to do, and now she cursed her luck for wasting the first two days at the Periyar Guest House. As she explored the garden, she spotted two tree houses; the rest were huts, randomly arranged. There was 'Layla' emanating from one of the huts, and she gingerly walked towards it, feeling a bit like a curious cat. A figure lay on the bed in a pair of shorts, smoking a cigarette, tapping his feet. It was Roger (or Roja, as Shaju called him).

He had been right there all the time and she hadn't known it.

She tried not to sound too excited, 'Oh look, we meet again! Do you live here?'

'Yes,' he said. He looked a tad embarrassed, and as if to explain, said, 'It's simple and basic. I don't need much.'

'No, it's lovely,' said Kavya.

They spent the next hour chatting. He was clean shaven today and that highlighted the blueness of his eyes. He was much taller than she remembered him, and much leaner too. She couldn't help gazing at his bare torso and tanned shoulders, thinking how fit he looked. She found out he was Swedish, that his last name was Nyström, that he came to Kerala every year and spent four to six months, that he didn't like the cold of northern Europe. That he last worked as a caregiver in an old people's home while back in Sweden. That he didn't know what job he would go back to. Maybe he would paint houses for a while, or tend gardens. She didn't know what it was, but she felt calm just being around him.

'How long are you in Kumily?' he broke her reverie. Her mind was painting pictures of a little girl with curls and blue eyes. Shut up, she told her mind.

'Just two more days,' she said.

'Have you been for a plantation walk yet?'

'No, I had signed up with the Forest Guest House, but I cancelled. I don't want to meet those antakshari monsters again.'

'What's ant-akshury?'

His non-Indianness suddenly struck her. 'Well, it's a song-chain game. You sing a song and the next person has to start a song with the last syllable of your song.'

He looked half-amused and half-intrigued. She prepared to leave. 'I must get going now.'

'I can take you for the plantation walk. I know this place well. You will be happy,' he said.

'Okay,' she said, excited at the prospect of a private tour. Impulse had won again.

They walked a lot together in the next two days. It didn't cross her mind to ask him about his family or childhood or who his friends were. Or what his degree was about, what else had he done for work—things that would tell her how financially sound he was. They were busy talking about tea and spices and soil and plantations and butterflies and leeches and mud and brick homes and another way of life. They were too busy eating dosas or a rice plate at Muthu's. Or navigating puddles, Roger out-Raleighing Sir Walter.

And then she had to leave. She had promised her friend Radhika that she would spend two days with her in Trichur before heading to Alleppey. She was to leave the next morning, but she didn't want to go. It was unusually windy that night and she squeezed his hand before they reached her hotel to let him know he would be missed.

'Come back soon,' he said, as she boarded the bus the next day.

'I will,' she replied. She didn't know how, but she wanted to.

'I will write to you. You can send me letters at Coffee Inn. Shaju will give them to me.'

She scribbled her hostel address on a piece of paper and gave it to him. With her telephone number. And her room number.

There were two letters and one postcard in her letterbox by the time she reached Bombay. Suddenly she felt like one of those girls whose family or boyfriend lived in another city and they eagerly checked the box every day and often looked disappointed.

Sometimes, there was a vanilla pod in the letter, sometimes a few coffee beans, sometimes a cutting on mangoes from *The Hindu*'s Sunday Folio magazine. But mostly, there was love and longing, the desire to meet again. The phone calls soon followed.

'Room no 614. Kavya! Call for you,' someone on the floor would bellow. The calls were transferred through the intercom from the mainline downstairs. There was one phone per floor, which means you had to run if you were at the other end of the corridor. Some girls would just be pacing up and down the corridor after

8.30 pm when there would be a flurry of calls. Magic hour, rates were halved then. Roger however called in the mornings, usually before she left for work. She had taken up a part-time gig with an agency; she hated the job, but the money was good, and if she wanted to travel…

They were soon making plans to meet again. She would call him every Monday at Kerala Spices, the spice shop across the road from Coffee Inn that belonged to his friend Varughese. 'Good evening, Kerala Spices,' his voice would beam from the phone, as she sat next to it every night, from 8.30 to 9.30 p.m. waiting for her to call, and hence intercepting all calls, as Varughese patiently waited for him to finish so he could shut shop and go home. Coffee Inn didn't have a phone then, as Shaju didn't believe he wanted to be accessible any more than he was. If anyone wanted him, they had to come find him.

By the time she returned to Coffee Inn a month later, they were a couple. And the tree house, their love nest. Varughese of Kerala Spices was like a local guardian, and Shaju came close to being best man. But these were figures in a hazy background. In the foreground: Roger and Kavya and the long conversations they had. They talked about a life together in the hills of Kerala. He could buy some land, grow coffee or spices. Even vanilla, which seemed to be in great demand. Kerala Spices had additional space in their shop where Kavya could sell city kitsch. Or start an organic shop, with a salad and smoothies bar. Maybe even a library or bookshop. She started painting dreams.

He told her about Katherine, his ex-girlfriend of nine years, his alcoholic and abusive father who had died, his estranged brother, who was on the sea somewhere and his mother who was his only family in the world.

November was a colder, wetter Thekkady, but one where she and Roger spent hours cooking, making mixed tapes, walking, looking at patches of land and building imaginary houses, talking about a kitsch store and salad bar that she could run (he would bring in the white people), imagining him as leading a group of chartered tourists. Listening to John Fogerty. Dancing. Making love.

They travelled to Munnar for a few days, as he wanted to get away from Thekkady for a while as people had already started talking about him and Kavya. She didn't like it; it made her feel like a tourist again. She had already started thinking of Thekkady as home.

They spent a few days in Trichur, hosted by Radhika's father, C.V. Mohan. Roger and CV (as he liked to be called) bonded over Kalyani beer and their love for the garden. Kavya was happy. He fitted in so well with the people who mattered. He also made travel look like therapy. As for her, the Konkan Railway's Netravati Express became a lifeline. She learnt to pack light and thrive on WL and RAC, acronyms for Waiting List and Reservation against Confirmation that would become part of her life in the next year or so. She made friends with Lokmanya Tilak Terminus (in the boondocks of Kurla where the train originated,) and side upper (her favourite berth). But it was also the line that drew her away from him.

By December, she loved him enough to want her best friend to like him. A Bangalore rendezvous had to be planned. He had to meet Shaili. She has to like him, Kavya thought. She was on sideupper again, this time to Bangalore on the Udyan Express. Indian Railways really owed her a frequent-flyer pass.

Shaili thought he was really nice, with a wicked sense of humour.

She thought they looked good together. That he was good for her. And she, for him. Shaili did ring a few alarm bells in Kavya's head. She asked all the questions friends are wont to ask: are you thinking long-term? In the hills? What will you do for a living in the hills? Have you met his family? Kavya realized that she still hadn't asked the bigger questions but she didn't want to kill the moment with money talk. They spent the next few days in Mysore at the Ritz, reliving the colonial era, in their room with a large four-poster bed and a bathroom the size of a Bombay apartment. It was quaint. It was nice. They went to Coorg a few days later, and brought in the New Year in their balcony in the Orange County resort on a moonless night, dancing to Fogerty.

It was her best new year ever.

In February, he asked her to marry him. 'I don't have much, but we can have a nice life together, Kavi,' he said. 'You pretend to be the city girl, but both you and I like it simple,' he said. He did it nicely, with a platter of a hibiscus flower and some shells on a sarong he spread out on Gokarna Beach. Behind the outline of his figure, the sun was setting.

'Yes,' she said, urgently and yet as if she had been expecting it all along. 'But you have to meet my family.' And then the real-time questions arose. 'But what about my job? Where will we live? Will you move to India? I don't like the cold.'

He had no answers. 'Give me some time,' he said. 'I'm working on a few things. I want my princess to be happy.'

It was the first time someone had called her a princess. It was the first time she felt like one.

'Will you come and meet my parents before you leave for Sweden? It's important to me,' she said.

'If that's what you want. Although I don't like big cities,' he replied.

Hosting Roger in Bombay was harder than she thought. It was like bringing a wild animal to a zoo. It was just March, but the heat was already palpable. Now she knew why she kept making the dash to the hills to see him despite friends warning her that 'the relationship has to be on your turf too'. Her friend Beena found him a hotel near her hostel; in Colaba, it was ironically called Greens. He could spend two nights there and then she could move him to her friend's place in Goregaon in the suburbs before he met her parents. He liked Beena—her easy charm, her non-intrusive warmth.

'You have nice friends,' he told Kavya.

The first bit of culture shock came in the way of a water-filled balloon hurled at his cheek as they travelled by autorickshaw from Goregaon station to her friends Bhushan and Anusha on the day of Holi. The interrogations began, even though Kavya had warned all her friends that they were not to court-martial him. They meant well. Kavya had been a serial singleton for a long time, her friends were concerned about her new love interest for whom she seemed willing to give up pretty much everything.

'Do they have any Indians in Sweden?'

'How come Ikea got so big?'

'Have you met Bjorn Borg?'

And then, inevitably: 'Why do you want to leave Europe and move to India of all places?'

He flinched at each question. She could see that. But she could also see how it might feel to be in his place: to be surrounded by aliens he badly wanted to adopt.

The meeting with Raj and Amu was better. They were the artsy types, used to listening to their hearts. They knew what it took to follow your dream, and were totally fascinated by his vision and passion. It's going well, Kavya thought. What her friends thought had always mattered to her.

And then of course: her parents. Roger brought some vanilla pods and some spices with him and her South Indian family, initially disturbed by his whiteness, began to feel at ease. Her father was a son of the soil and his ears usually perked up at the mention of the word 'land'.

'So have you purchased the land for your coffee plantation?' he asked. Kavya had told her parents he was going to grow coffee.

'No, but I have a few friends, they are helping me out,' he said.

'Is it legal for foreigners to buy land in India?' her father asked.

'There are ways around that, I am told.'

A few questions about family and Sweden and her father began to hold forth on the Swedish glass blowers. Kavya sensed that the important thing was still left to be discussed.

'Amma, I think we should have the wedding when Roger returns from Sweden, in June,' she said.

'You will have to give us a list of who is coming from your side, so we can make arrangements,' said her father, in the manner of the father of the bride.

'Don't worry about that. There won't be too many people.'

And that was that.

Suddenly, it was real and not so much fun anymore. Bringing Roger to Bombay seemed to have distorted the magical bubble she was living in. She couldn't put a finger on it, but she felt a palpable unease from that day on. They went through the motions of their relationship as before. As if the Bombay chapter was something that never happened. In April, she was to meet him again. 'Get down at Devikulam junction this time,' he said. 'I want to show you a magical place.'

This was Santhanpara, thirty kilometres from Munnar, a place of coffee and quiet. It was where they were going to make their home, he had decided. He had been coming here for the last two months to escape what he called 'the excesses of Thekkady and Munnar'. Kavya was confused. *Excesses? Munnar?* She didn't want to be a princess on an island. Santhanpara was like being marooned. There was no one in sight, no signs of activity, except the Coffee Institute, where his friend Doraikannu worked as an office assistant and his wife worked as a cleaner.

Besides, she had begun to like Thekkady. She could imagine living there. She had already made friends. She liked Varughese and his wife, Shaju and some of his friends, the lady who worked at the arts and crafts shop outside Periyar.

And now this. 'But why don't you want to live in Thekaddy? They are so nice, those people!'

'No Kavya, trust me, I have a plan. I found this beautiful piece of land at the edge of the cliff. It is so stunning. You can only see mountains 360 degrees.'

'But who comes here? How will we sell our stuff? What about my café?'

'You know something? In five years, Thekkady will be finished. And then people will want places like these.'

'But this place doesn't even have a hotel or a resort,' she pointed out. Did she have to? she wondered. After all, they were staying at the quarters provided to Doraikannu by the Coffee Institute.

'People are buying land here, Kavi. The land is gold. Places will come up. You'll see!'

'I don't have five years. I want it now!' the little girl in her wanted to cry.

As the days went by, she saw meaning in his plan. It was about entering a new market rather than a saturated market. It was about starting slow. It was about building assets. But she still felt alone and lonely in the larger scheme of things. Meanwhile, Doraikannu and his wife and their utter simplicity had begun to grow on her. She could see herself getting an academic gig at the Coffee Institute. That Master's degree in biochemistry could finally come in handy.

May and June were letter-filled months. Roger was in Sweden, a home he never felt at home in. He sent postcards with watercolours of luscious fruit and flowers of spring, and the letters were longer, more poignant, more about hope and the future and the belief that it would all go well. They did speak on the phone a few times, but neither could afford the cost of international calls and there was the time difference. She also thought this was the best time to consolidate work, find out if she could work on a few freelance projects from Santhanpara.

The internet had just seeped into people's lives, although Roger was light-years away from anything to do with a computer. But Munnar would definitely have the internet, because of the tourists, she figured. So maybe she could…

Slowly but surely, she started packing her things, sorting stuff, figuring out what it was she really needed. She was going to lead a life of minimalism and it made her happy that she was clearing up her clutter.

Roger returned to Kerala in July. She couldn't bear the thought that she wouldn't meet him before the wedding, set for August 27, as her mother couldn't find an auspicious date earlier. So in July, she made a last trip to Santhanpara and took a few things along—her books, some things for the house, clothes and linen, a lamp she loved. She was setting up home finally, and it was a nice feeling. Roger was more preoccupied than usual. He spoke less, was out more. She brushed it all off as pre-wedding blues.

The land deal was more convoluted than he thought, and Doraikannu was not as influential as he had held himself out to be. Kavya lent Roger fifteen thousand rupees, as he said he was short.

'The money will come in from Sweden,' he assured her. She didn't think to ask how much he had already, who had promised what, how much of his own he had invested. She didn't think it appropriate to ask. But she did see the land, and yes, the view was truly magical. She had already started placing her things in the house, planned the kitchen, the dining area. She had always wanted an open kitchen, and a vegetable patch in her backyard. Now she would have it.

Every time she returned to Bombay, her life in the city seemed thinner and less fulfilling and she yearned to return to the hills. Just one more month, she thought. When Roger called her the next time, it was end July, and he mentioned something about going to Sri Lanka.

'I have to renew my visa,' he said. Sri Lanka was the best option, as it was the closest, and he had to leave the country once. It suddenly struck her that he was on a tourist visa and she wondered whether that would have any implication on his moving to India permanently or buying land or doing business.

'No worries. He's marrying you, right? He acquires your status,' a friend told her.

That easy? Maybe it was. Maybe luck was on her side.

She didn't hear from him for the next two weeks. Somewhere she registered that this was odd, it had never happened before, however busy he had been. He was due to leave for Sri Lanka on August 2, so she thought he might call her around then. Nothing.

The wait was getting longer, and so was the unease. Kavya had given up her room at the hostel and moved back into her parents' home. She thought it would be nice to spend time with them before she moved away.

Roger was supposed to arrive on August 12, so they could do the last-minute wedding arrangements together. The cards had already been sent out, the venue booked, the menu decided, the caterers paid. Kavya wanted to discuss the decor and floral arrangements with Roger, and so decided to wait for him. Her wedding sari—a mango-yellow Paithani with gold motifs sighed softly at her when she looked at it in her closet. Her mother chose a raw silk churidar kurta with a jacket for Roger. 'He is so fair…he will look so nice in this,' she had said.

Still no call.

Kavya was getting restless and worried, but managed to hide it from her family. Gift envelopes and cards had started to arrive from the friends who wouldn't be able to make it. One was from his mother, it had two hundred dollars in it.

Finally, on August 17th, there was a call from Kerala. It wasn't Roger. It was C.V. Menon from Trichur. 'Kavya, are you all right, my child?'

CV always had this daddy thing about him, the power to sense and fix things, make things all right.

'Yes, Uncle. Why do you ask?'

'Roger is here. He arrived last night by train. He looks strange. I think there's a problem.'

Wedding in ten days. This was not sounding good. 'What problem, Uncle? Tell me everything,' she pleaded.

'He looks severely dehydrated and he has lost a lot of weight. Something seems to have happened. Here, talk to him.'

It was Roger. But he didn't sound the same.

'Kavi, how are you, my love?'

'I am fine. What is Uncle saying? What happened?'

'You know Kavi, I think Doraikannu is trying to kill me. I saw him mixing something in my food and I asked him about it and then he got all abusive. And then one time, I think he tried to give me an injection when I was sleeping and I caught him.'

Nothing was making sense.

'But I thought you were in Sri Lanka.'

'I think the people at the airport were all his friends because they were looking at me in a strange way. The lady on the aircraft added something to my drink. I am sure Kavi. They are all in it together. Varughese had told me once that he had people in Sri Lanka.'

'But how can that be, Roger? He's your friend. Why would he do this to you?'

'I think he wants to take over my land.'

'You just relax, okay? Everything will be fine. Just get here. We have a wedding in ten days.'

CV came back on the line. It was the first time he spoke in Malayalam.

'I am putting him on a train as soon as I get a confirmed ticket. I will let you know the arrival details. Just be there to receive him. But take someone with you. Look after yourself,' he said.

Alarm bells. Alarm bells. Worst-case scenario? She was already in problem-fixing mode. She called Doraikannu. He sounded distressed.

'I think Roger is having many problems. You are like my sister, so I want to tell you. I think the tribal people gave him magic mushrooms, maybe. When he came back from Thekkady, he was shouting at me that day and asking for his money. I don't have any money. My wife is pregnant and he was making nuisance in my house. So I told him to go away.'

'How long has he been like this?'

'I don't know. One-two months maybe. But you be careful, sister,' he said.

More alarm bells.

By the time she called Varughese, she already knew what he would say.

'He was like my brother. And he was saying so much bad things. That Doraikannu poisoned his mind about me, I am thinking.'

Who was right? Who should she believe? She tried reaching Shaju through Varughese, but he refused to speak to her. She could never piece together what happened between July 30th and August 17th, because every version of it was a blur. But one thing was clear. The universe was conspiring to protect her from the man she loved.

One version: someone fed Roger magic mushrooms in Thekkady. Maybe it was Shaju or Varughese. Maybe it was in jest. Maybe it was a conspiracy against the white man who wanted to buy land and settle there. The mushrooms triggered off a series of episodes. It transformed him into an angry, ranty, suspicious man. It tested his friendship with Shaju. They fell apart. He went to Sri Lanka in that state. The rest was disaster.

ROGER, OVER AND OUT

Another version: Roger had always been delusional and paranoid and managed to hide it from her. Or she hadn't wanted to see it. Kavya had been so much in love with him that she failed to see the signs.

Version three: Roger's dole was under threat in Sweden. He badly wanted to move to Kerala. The only way he could survive was if he married smart. So he tricked Kavya into falling in love with him, because once he was married to an Indian woman, he was legally safe.

He called the next day. 'I thought you were supposed to be on a train,' she said, panicking. CV had called to tell her he had boarded S5 on Mangala Express.

'Kavi, I think they are trying to kill me.'

'Who? Who's trying to kill you?'

'Your people. Your father's people. They followed me to Sri Lanka, and now they are on my train. I saw one of them signalling to the guard, so I got off.'

'Roger, please get back on the train. The sooner you reach me, the safer you will be. I beg of you!' she pleaded.

'Okay Kavi, I trust you.'

Her mind was processing the information way too fast. Who should she call? It had to be someone medical. The only person she could think of was her childhood friend Sujata. She still hadn't told her about Roger. And now she had to know everything.

Sujata was a doctor, a radiologist. She was well connected and knew a lot of people in the medical fraternity. She was also the kind of person who liked to take charge. She had always been skeptical about Kavya's bohemian lifestyle, particularly after she had shown up at her doctor's quarters one night with her then actor-boyfriend, asking if they could spend the night. Kavya didn't want to be judged again, so she had kept Roger a secret from Sujata.

But now she had to tell her. And Sujata said, 'I told you so!' with a wealth of satisfaction in her voice. She read Kavya a little lecture, reminding her that it paid to be prudent and that adventure was not for everyone.

'When is he coming?' she asked.

'He arrives tomorrow noon, by train. I don't know what to do with him.'

'Bring him to my house. We can pretend we are having a pre-wedding bash. I can call my psychotherapist friend Dr Sushant Gupta to suss the situation out. Just call a few friends over to make it real. They'll show up, it's your wedding. But don't tell them anything. Make it look natural. We should not alarm him in any way.'

Sujata's clinical mind was already working overtime. But Kavya was grateful she had friends who could think on their feet. She didn't know if she could have thought of all this herself. Because she was in love. Because the man she was in love with was…what was happening to him? Because she had a wedding to plan. Because. This was Roger, how could he harm her, the same gentle Roger who carried her over puddles and sent her coffee beans?

The next afternoon, Kavya and her brother Ravi went to pick up Roger at Thane station. When she saw him, her heart sank. CV was right. He looked like a drug-destroyed beach bum, gaunt, at least ten kilos thinner than when she had last seen him. His clothes added to the impression: a frayed T-shirt and a pair of cargoes that had seen better days.

'Thank God you're here, Kavi. This train was so scary.'

She had been reading up on magic mushrooms and making a mental tick at every symptom he seemed to reveal. Hallucinations. Check. Delusions. Check.

He reached out to her for some contact. She pretended to be preoccupied with shooing off the porter. The alarm bells were now tolling a death knell.

'Come, we are going to a safe place,' she told him and already she heard another tone in her voice, a motherly tone. 'No one will bother you there.' Already her body was saying: This is the first time you haven't hugged him.

Sujata's house proved to be a blessing, because he had a room to himself and it was so much easier than taking him home in that state. Kavya hadn't told her brother anything yet, but it didn't take him long to piece things together on their journey from the railway station.

She had managed to get twelve confirmations to the spontaneous sangeet bash on Uma's terrace. Snacks were ordered, a dhol was arranged, and her brother would play DJ. Roger was left alone most of the afternoon, with food being served in the room. Kavya suddenly felt like a conspirator when Dr Sushant Gupta arrived in the evening.

'Don't worry,' he assured her, after he heard Kavya's story. 'I have seen lot of cases like this. I will handle him.'

Roger claimed he lost his suitcase on the train, and only had a small haversack with his immediate belongings, but no clothes. Kavya went out and bought him a shirt and trousers and some underwear for the evening. He could always wear her dad's old clothes later, she thought. *Later?*

The friends began to arrive. They started out exuberant and

cheerful—this was a sangeet, after all—but almost immediately, they began to sense the palpable tension on that terrace, as they danced to 'Choli ke peeche kya hai', orchestrated hellos and hugs, and tried to keep the wedding camaraderie going. Kavya tried to play the bashful bride but she knew she was trying too hard, she was watching Roger all the time, praying that the doctors would laugh at her fears and declare he was fine. But Roger was not himself, and distinctly uncomfortable. When her friends asked—and many of them did—she said it was jet lag. She didn't know that by the time her friends got home that night, they had already read the subtexts.

Dr Gupta managed a few moments with Kavya.

'It's not looking good. We have to run some tests though. I suggest you get him admitted at Mhaskar Hospital. I will organize the formalities. He can't be here.'

She was sinking. She had to tell her parents now. The wedding was three days away.

'I think you should call it off,' said Sujata, in her problem-solving voice. 'There are too many unknowns, and it will take a long time to figure things out without a medical history. Plus, he can't even be here beyond 2nd September, as his visa expires.'

He had gone to Sri Lanka to renew it, no? Had they refused him an extension? Or had he not tried? Had he gone at all? And how did Sujata know this? Had she checked his passport? How dare she?

Did she dare to feel outrage at Sujata? At Roger? What did she feel?

Kavya only knew that she could feel control of her life slipping away. Other people had taken charge. Roger was admitted to Mhaskar Hospital where he was put on tranquilizers and tested for drugs, amphetamine and AIDS, among other things. He tested negative. They ran an MRI scan. Nothing.

ROGER, OVER AND OUT

Dr Gupta asked the questions straight. How long had she known him? What was he doing in Australia? Sri Lanka? Why did he come to Kerala every year? Suddenly, her answers lacked conviction.

'I think he has delusions. It happens a lot to paranoid schizophrenics,' he announced.

Schizophrenic? Roger? How? How could she not have sensed it?

'But how is it possible that I haven't seen anything in the nine months that I've known him. There would have been some symptom. Something that would have been amiss.'

She was looking for hope. Desperate, can't-give-up-on-love hope.

'Well, either he was very clever at camouflaging it, or something has happened to trigger a series of episodes in the recent past. But it's difficult to be sure without his medical history. Do you really want to go that far?'

Time was running out. What about his visa? Should she call someone in Sweden? She didn't know the language. One attempt to speak to his mother resulted in nothing as she didn't speak or understand a word of English. The Swedish embassy was not much help either.

And then there was the wedding. Of course she couldn't go through the wedding. Not in this state. Maybe never. She had to make calls. Inform people. Where was the list?

She called home to ask her mother to locate the list of invitees and their numbers. Each one was called and informed the wedding was off due to a medical emergency. 'There's no need to explain anything, Amma,' she said. What she did not know was that by this time word had got around that Kavya had a psycho boyfriend; anyone who was remotely connected to her life knew. But it was not something she had to deal with now.

Roger spent the next few days in Mhaskar Hospital, pacing like a restless cat, waiting for Kavya to arrive every morning. She spent her nights at Sujata's, unable to sleep, adding and subtracting details, but never getting anywhere. Some nurses told her he had refused medication, saying that he was getting married in a few days and that he would invite them as well.

Kavya had to arrange for him to go back to Sweden. The hospital bills were mounting and her savings evaporating. Roger felt helpless, and promised he would pay her back. He offered her his Olympus camera. 'Keep this, Kavi, it will be some money. I am sorry I am making you do all this. But I am really feeling better. I am sure I will be okay by the wedding.'

She told him there would be no wedding. She told him that the doctors had advised him to go back, get treated and get better. She broke his spirit but he tried not to show it. 'Our time will come, Kavi,' was all he said, and hugged her tight. It was a really bad moment, but she remembered she hadn't given him his mother's card and the two hundred dollars and handed them over.

She hadn't been home ever since Roger returned. Now she knew she had to go home and face her family. She had prepared herself for it, readied herself to defend Roger and her love for him, what they had meant. She wondered whether they would be silent about it because her family was good at silence, at leaving things unsaid but hanging in the air.

There was a deathly silence when she arrived. It was a Sunday. Ravi and her dad were watching a cricket match. Her sister Revati had stepped out for a walk. Amma was in the kitchen, cooking. Her family didn't do hugs, she knew that, but a hug would have really done it for her. Instead Appa just lowered the TV volume and asked her, 'How is he?'

She was grateful; she hadn't expected them to care. The question softened her. 'He's getting better, but they have to send him back, as we don't have any medical history, and it will take a while to treat him.'

'Where is his family? How come no one is bothered?'

Okay, here it comes, she thought. 'I don't know, Appa,' she said.

'You don't know? Hah… coffee plantation! Spice business! Handicrafts shop! Bloody scamster! I knew something was fishy,' and he slammed the door and walked out.

Her brother Ravi didn't say a word. Her sister Revati had just returned from her walk. She gripped her shoulder and said, 'I will do reiki for you.'

Suddenly a conversation with a skeptical cousin came back to her. This one was Li'l Ms. Right, always doing the right thing— marriage at twenty-four, baby at twenty-six, job and house in Dubai. She had come to visit Kavya because she wouldn't be able to make it to the wedding. Kavya could sense an unhealthy curiosity. LMR was fishing for too many details. Where was this plantation? Who would they sell the coffee to? How would they survive till the first crop was ready? Kavya was getting uncomfortable and told her, 'It is obvious that you don't dream.' LMR looked hurt and said, 'I'm not jealous of you. I'm only concerned.' They were never to speak again.

Amma was softer. 'You're just going through shanidosha. I know your heart is pure. God is there. He will make it all right. *But why did you have to do this, Krishna?*' she demanded of her favourite god. Her voice cracked. Kavya flinched. She hadn't heard her mother break down in a long time.

She realized that she needed to heal before she returned to her parents' home. She had to reapply to the hostel. Could she have her room back? she wondered. Her head was too full of logistics to grieve.

Meanwhile, a friend, Mona, who worked for a travel agency, had arranged a ticket to Copenhagen, the nearest airport to Helsingborg, where he lived. Scandinavian Airlines was alerted that he was on medication and had to be looked after. The day his flight was to depart was Ganpati immersion day, and ordinarily Kavya would have never stepped out in that din. But somehow the drums and revelry outside the taxi seemed nothing compared to the noise in her head. As the taxi drew closer to the airport, her heart started beating really fast. What if something goes wrong and the flight is cancelled? Or he refuses to leave? What if there's a scene at the airport? She had never wanted to run away from someone more. But she had never loved someone more either. Roger held her hand tightly as they pulled closer to the departure gate. Something told her she should not hold him back. He might read that as hope.

They got off the taxi and she handed him his ticket and passport. 'Take care. And write to me soon, okay?' she said, in the most everyday nothing-much-happening voice she could muster. They stared at each other for a while, each knowing that they would never see the other, whatever they might say now. When he could stand it no more, he hugged her. She let him. She was crying inside, wailing, an Irene Pappas Greek tragedy howl of rage and sorrow inside, but on her face, there were no tears. And before she knew it, he was gone. She could have waited till he vanished from sight, but she just turned around and kept walking.

'Someone out there loves you,' Dr Gupta had said on the day of Roger's discharge, handing her an envelope that was marked

ROGER, OVER AND OUT

'Medical Report of Roger Nyström'. 'Keep it,' he added. 'It may be needed.' She knew what the envelope would contain, but she still read the three-page deconstruction of the man she loved, her fingers quivering as she held them. 'Thank God you found out before the wedding,' he had added, as she bid him goodbye.

She tried very hard to believe that was true, but she couldn't. Maybe she had forsaken her only chance at real love. Fifteen years later, she could still catch herself wondering: how bad could it have been if she had gone ahead?

She was in therapy for the next six months. And Alprax. Lots of it. Finally, she gave up both, because they were holding her back. She returned to the hostel and decided to start all over again. The letters started coming, but this time they were letters of despair, about undergoing therapy, about feeling debilitated by drugs, about feeling lonely. One day, she stopped opening them and they went straight to the bin. With them, Kavya's princess moment, her café dreams and that open kitchen. But the puddle still gleams sometimes in her memory.

IN MY MOTHER'S SHADOW

Annabelle Furtado

19 March 2011

A phone is ringing. I'm asleep. I come awake and I know immediately, instinctively that it is bad news. No one would call at 3:40 a.m. Not in our family. We've lived in several time zones so we're used to waiting for a reasonable hour to call. This is news that can't wait.

'What is it?' I demand, when I finally find my mobile phone in the darkness of our bedroom in Kuwait.

'You know how Mummy was breathless yesterday right, and she's been complaining that she's tired for the past few days…'

'Yes, yes, get to it,' is my silent plea. I'm expecting my sister to tell me that our mother needs to be hospitalized—something mother always dreaded.

'Well, we rushed her to the hospital, but it was too late. She—just passed away.' My sister begins to sob.

How can she be dead? I spoke to her, what, eight hours ago? Dead? Just like that?

THAT NIGHT WAS a pivotal point in my life. It still gives me the shivers four years on. After that phone call I might as well have lived in a walk-in refrigerator. Voices kept me busy. I responded. Things had to be done. I did them. But I was numb and perhaps even on guard. With our mother gone, what would happen? Everything, it seemed to me, would fall apart.

When I got to India the next day, things seemed unreal. My father, nearly eighty, seemed utterly alone, despite having six of his seven children around. My siblings seemed to me as if they were lost and confused. While I comforted family members and virtual strangers whose lives had been touched by my mother, I forgot to grieve.

The previous months had not been easy on us as a family. At the time of my mother's death, one of my sisters had already spent three months in a mental health institution in Bangalore. After many years of disagreements, bitter battles and too many wars of words, we had, as siblings, decided that it was best for our sister to be taken care of by professionals.

This had not been an easy decision. We had to worry about our parents and how they would face the extended family (the social stigma to mental illness in India being so great). All that apart, the mere logistics were difficult. It took us a year to coordinate everything. To find out as much as we could about the place, its repute and if the doctors there really knew what they were doing. Convincing our parents that this was for the greater good had taken even longer. My mother, the large-hearted woman that she was, could only see this as a failure on her part. We tried to make her understand: we were my sister's flesh and blood, too, and we couldn't bear to see how much she was hurting mother with her illness.

The siblings contributed to pay for our sister's medication

and accommodation. And yet the biggest challenge lay ahead. That was to get my sister from Mumbai to Bangalore without a fight.

Mother's faith always left me at loggerheads with my own. I did not understand why she had to go all the way to Mahim or Sion from Borivali (one hour of travel either way by train) for consecutive months at the crack of dawn to offer prayers for 'everyone's intentions' at sacred shrines. She was praying for all of us. Of course, being almost the youngest, my opinion on the subject rarely mattered. But then, in times of crisis, like this one, her faith came to our rescue as well. I believe that my parents could not have made that difficult road trip from Mumbai to Bangalore in their old age without God's grace.

When they finally arrived in Bangalore in December the previous year, my sister did not go gracefully at first. So it was nothing short of a miracle that she finally agreed that the home in Bangalore would do her good. For my mother, it was the final battle which she felt she had lost, though she later told me that she had a few months of peace because of this decision.

Two of my sisters battled with depression. Fortunately only one was in complete denial that she needed help.

When my mother and I called my sister in the home to inquire about her well-being, both of them broke down. The distance had done them good but it was a terribly difficult conversation that I won't easily forget. It broke my heart.

Now, I took on the task of bringing my sister back for my mother's funeral. In fear of her taking the news badly I couldn't tell her the truth till we reached the front door. I made a mental note to finish my sobbing before meeting my sister who was overjoyed that she was returning home. Of course when the news was broken, she didn't easily forgive me for keeping things secret.

WHEN MY FIRST child was born in 2006, a dear friend called from overseas to congratulate me. I was too preoccupied with baby duties to talk. Mother simply smiled and said to the friend on the other end of the line, 'Well, her hands are full dear, she is a mother now.' There was a mix of bittersweet sarcasm in her voice that day which still echoes in my mind.

I became a mother for the second time eleven months before my mother passed away in 2011. On both occasions, I could tell from her eyes, the empathy she felt while I was in labour. I guess we were finally on an equal turf. She said she didn't expect us to have as many children as she did but that she was hopeful that we'd share the joys of motherhood. She truly believed that all of it had been a joy, despite the pain and trouble some of our lives must have caused her.

Whenever we teased her to name a favourite from her seven, she'd always tell us that she had carried all of us for an equal term and that she loved us all equally.

She was our anchor. Four years have passed since her demise. I don't blame her for leaving us so suddenly. I only wish I could pick up the phone and tell her how bad things got since she left. Of course I am not the first to have lost a parent, I'm just someone whose life altered drastically when it happened.

Treating my parents as his own, my husband had had the foresight to invite my mother overseas for a break in February 2011. This was just a month before she would leave us forever. Theirs wasn't your typical mother-in-law and son-in-law relationship. They had their differences but remained extremely fond of each other. When he insisted that mother visit us in Kuwait, I knew she would come up with a thousand reasons to avoid the trip. But she proved me wrong and I am so grateful she was with us.

For the first time in my life, I saw my mother use a wheelchair on her return to Mumbai. It was also the last time I saw her alive as well. Over twenty-five years of high diabetes had taken a toll on her tired feet and she complained about not being as quick as before. Before she travelled back to India, as was her usual style, she stocked my fridge with good food and great love.

I remember walking around my apartment in a daze on the morning of her passing, wondering if she had ever left when memories of her were so fresh in my house.

A few month's later, on mother's birthday that year, I decided to bring out the pork sorpotel gravy she had prepared for us. 'Since it is cooked in vinegar, it remains good in the freezer,' she had said to me. To partake of a meal prepared by his beloved, late wife of forty-eight years was the biggest gift my father received on my mother's birthday. I could see how much it affected him, rescuing him from sadness and confusion. From loneliness.

Perhaps that was the tipping point, because soon I became unstoppable, rushing from one task to the next as if I had forgotten the pause button. It was as if a huge grey cloud had passed over me and I couldn't see ahead.

We were about to relocate. So perhaps it was also the pressure that I was going to move to another country soon. The task of finding a new school for my three-year-old in the middle of the year and setting up a new house was making me quite anxious.

Of course we had done it twice before. But being a stay-at-home mother for over four years had made me less sure of myself and I had grown to resent my life in Kuwait. I also missed close friends.

So much had changed after that night-time phone call. I lived in a state of vague dread. Things that I could handle easily before seemed to have the power to take me apart. I was always on guard.

I found it hard to sleep. For a few days I walked about in a daze feeling super powerful and oddly, at the same time, extremely anxious about the most basic things. I went for longer walks than usual. Listened to loud music to motivate me on the walks and argued relentlessly about non issues. Luckily my eldest sister and my husband helped. They are the anchors who brought me back to shore. Through my outbursts I could tell that something was just not right. Only I didn't know what it was at the time. I took to writing and made endless gratitude lists but they didn't help.

I found myself unable to comprehend things and constantly worried that the world was coming to an end. Around this time, two young college students, Keenan Santos and Reuben Fernandez, were ruthlessly murdered in my home town, Mumbai, for standing up to goons for their female friends. Though I was not connected to the story, I spent a long night writing about it on my blog and got needlessly worked up. I badly needed to disconnect.

The grey cloud prevented me from seeing what I was doing. My children were young but they sensed something was wrong. My husband and my elder sister tried their best and then one day, suddenly, I looked, really looked into my husband's anxious teary eyes and realized that something was wrong.

With me.

I couldn't believe that I had psyched myself into this mess. I went with my husband to the psychiatry ward of the biggest hospital there was and he talked the doctor into not admitting me. Somehow he kept me out of there and in return, I agreed that I would take my medication faithfully.

A few months of this helped get me back on track. I wanted to believe that I didn't need it, but I didn't resist because I knew that at that point all I needed was sleep. I couldn't believe how little I had been sleeping. I had been running on empty and I had driven my family to the brink too.

Some years later I interviewed an accomplished British tapping therapist who has treated many celebrities struggling with anxiety. He offered me a complimentary session and I told him I was struggling with guilt. I said I had subjected my family to an ordeal and that I had been diagnosed as bipolar. He refused to believe that I had bipolar disorder. Having healed countless people with various disorders, addictions and ailments, he was convinced that I was simply labelling myself for no good reason.

'I've seen many patients who are bipolar and they fluctuate all the time. Please put that diagnosis out of your head,' he said. 'You were merely responding to your mother's sudden death and you have nothing to feel guilty about.'

I like to believe the therapist was right. After all he was merely interested in the facts. That day I left his session more sure about myself.

There is no shame in telling my story. If it can help others understand that a breakdown doesn't mean you are dysfunctional, I stand to be heard.

And what of my sister, the one who had been persuaded to be treated in an institution? To her credit she decided to return to the home a few weeks after my mother's passing. She completed a year there and was employed at the facility while she was there.

THE GUILT AND anxiety I was feeling was compounded by the fact that two of my siblings had suffered from bipolar disorder for many years when I was in my twenties. It turned our world upside down. To my family's utter despair, when one sibling went into a manic state, the other followed suit. There were two people to deal with which made things even more complicated. It is something I do not wish on anyone or their families. Increasingly more and more people are discussing the issue and are willing to accept that it needs to be treated. But the situation is still bad, and it was much worse when my sisters were diagnosed as bipolar.

No one is merely crazy. We just don't know how to describe or treat the illness. The lines between normal and abnormal are often so personal. What may seem normal to one may be abnormal to another. Depression, post-partum depression, schizophrenia, bipolar disorder—these are all words I had heard time and again in psychology class. It never sunk in deeper than when these words were flung in my face at different points in my life when I took my sisters to get help.

There was little knowledge of the subject at the time, before the internet exploded with all the answers. In the 1990s one of the doctors in Mumbai prescribed such a strong sedative that my sister's entire body went stiff. A well-intentioned neighbour said that shock treatment would do the trick. When she read the horror on my face, she confessed, 'We did it for my brother. I know it is scary, but it may work.' We never took that route.

ANNABELLE FURTADO

I read reams about the subject from books and periodicals and watched singer Sinead O' Connor's interview on the subject. I prayed for a magic formula to make the disharmony go away. With the condition came endless arguments. Bitter and cold resentment and a house filled with unpredictable moments.

I believe we became stronger as a family with these events, but it also tore us apart. My brother was in high school at the time and he grew resentful towards both the sisters for acting the way they did. The most mundane issues would result in long drawn arguments. I turned to my friends who came to help at different points in time, with no questions asked. One helped convince one sister that she should board an ambulance, another made the same sibling believe a few years later that we were going on a long drive, when in fact we were on our way to the nursing home. We needed the support of young men because my sisters would become boisterous and difficult to handle when they were at their worst.

All these events took a huge toll on my mother, who was the subject of most of the attacks from one of my afflicted sisters. Mother would always break down wondering if she had failed in some way. After cruel words were flung across the room, we had to reassure her that all her children were not the same and that our sister needed help; that the bitter words used by my sister were the illness talking. During most of this time, the external family largely stood around and did nothing. Actually they did do something—they judged us. It was easy for anyone to believe this sister who was not well. She went around with a story of how my parents were ill-treating her and not finding her a suitor, when in fact they had tried every possible avenue to find her a life partner.

It was at this point that the rest of us siblings, now married and with our own children and families, had to step in and decide that my parents had clearly had enough. This was barely a few months before my mother passed away.

My illness made my love for my husband and my in-laws even stronger. His resolve to see us through this dark chapter together has given me immeasurable strength. Through long phone calls with siblings overseas, my husband and in-laws tried to comprehend what was going on. Almost overnight my in-laws left everything in India to be with us. Just seeing them in person switched on a light bulb in me which dispelled the darkness of the recent past.

Too many people aren't as blessed. I believe that the few years I had spent selflessly helping others came back in the form of these blessings. My hisaab was done. I've now learnt that it is okay to say no sometimes. That it is not so important to be the martyr all the time. That other people can be quick to judge you, but that's who they are and their judgments are their problem, not mine.

One of my six siblings said, 'Our mother's death never shook me as much as Annabelle's illness did.' Her sentiment has stayed with me. It reminds me that my life impacts so many, especially those that matter the most. I owe it to them all to get a grip on myself, to keep in the light.

DRIS

Manoj Menon

I AM SURE Dris meant nothing by it. He almost never did. He couldn't possibly have meant to stagger home hammered out of his wits, with his pants neatly slung over one hand, when her friends were visiting. You couldn't convince her of that though. My sister was certain that he did these things with the sole purpose of embarrassing her. Sonia can be quite pig-headed that way. Once she has formed an opinion of you, that's pretty much it. My brother? Madhu's different. He seemed to see a side to the man that the rest of us missed, or maybe he was seeing the man he wanted Dris to be. We were never quite sure.

When we were growing up, Dris was almost always wasted by the time we woke up and then he would go and drink some more. Being the kind of man who wasn't attached to money or much else, he was pretty content. I mean, happy content. You could put the man up at the Malabar Hotel or the Shanmugham Lodge and it would all be the same to him. He drank his tea, read his books (wrote a few too, but that is a story for another day), saw a whole lot of patients, all the time chugging Honeybee brandy. Putting meals on the table or paying school fees were not the kind of issues that held his attention. Mention the evolution of the communist movement in Kerala or the chances of a black pope, however, and you would have his undivided attention. Faith is a strange thing. His patients seemed to worship him and put their lives willingly in his very drunk hands. I once asked one of them why he would want to be treated by a very wasted doctor. The man said quite matter-of-factly that Dris had saved his father and that, drunk or not, he was the best doctor he had ever known.

Melodramatic as that may sound, there were quite a few chaps who felt that way. You see, while Dris was pretty iffy about his family, he was generosity personified to the average stranger. He could give you the clothes off his back if you asked him, and he probably did, considering that he had, on occasion, come home without his trousers. It was not that he was cold to us, but it never seemed that he cared about us very much. Come the needy stranger, though, and he would sponsor his child's education, take care of his medical expenses and pour his heart and wallet out without inhibition. Mind you, this was a man who never hugged us when we were growing up and most definitely didn't pay our school fees.

Amma was the one who held it all together. She paid our fees, put us through college and made sure we didn't miss school outings for lack of funds, all this on a school teacher's salary. She was an Economics professor in university before giving it all up to marry Dris and bring up his children. Now the thing about Amma was that she loved Dris. Crazy as it may sound, in spite of Dris not giving a hoot about his family, she remained devoted to him until his dying day. Dris wasn't always fun and games either. He had his abusive violent fits, as most alcoholics do. I guess she filed that away deep in her subconscious and chose only to see the goodness in him. Maybe she hung in there for us. Either way, she had our back in those crazy days.

The three of us remember our childhood very differently. It was almost like we lived different lives. My brother being the eldest bore the brunt of it, I guess. He had seen Dris during his glory days and watched him slip to his lowest depths. Being the eldest, he felt the need to protect his siblings from their crazy dad, which is not very easy to do when you are a ten-year-old. He made quite a fist of it though and was always our first line of defence. My sister dealt with it by cutting Dris out of her life. She didn't enjoy her childhood very much and I suspect was more than a little glad to leave home when college called. I am not quite sure how I dealt with it. Surprisingly, I remember my growing up as an exciting and eventful time. My sister has a theory that this is some sort of defence mechanism. That be as it may, one thing Dris ensured was that our lives would never be dull. I am not sure what issues plague the average eleven- and twelve-year-olds, but we were detectives growing up, trying to ferret out bottles of booze that Dris had stashed away all over the house so that he wouldn't be drunk when an uncle or a friend came over.

On one such monsoon day, our mother had entrusted us with the task of making sure that Dris stayed relatively sober until the afternoon as some uncle or the other was visiting. However, Dris somehow managed to give us the slip and as we huddled nervously under an umbrella outside the gate of our house wondering what to do, we saw an autorikshaw pull up at the outer entrance of the layout. There was this thirty-metre pathway leading from where the autorikshaw pulled up to where we were standing. Dris stepped out of the rikshaw and stood absolutely still under his umbrella, facing us. It seemed like forever that we stood at two ends of the pathway in the pouring rain, each waiting for the other to make a move. I remember my sister mentioning that if we didn't get to him fast, he would probably get back into the rikshaw and leave and then there was no telling what state he would come back in. I decided to make a dash for him; element of surprise and all that. Just as I started running towards him, Dris let go of his umbrella. The wind caught it and it went spiralling away like something out of a very bad Bollywood movie. I was half way to him now and Dris pulled out a bottle from his pocket. He flicked open the cap and put it to his mouth. It couldn't have taken more than a few seconds for me to reach him but somehow he managed to empty the half bottle of brandy down his throat in that time. We stood facing each other for a few seconds with only the sound of the pounding rain. Dris dropped the bottle, wiped his mouth with the back of his sleeve and strode past me towards the house with a smirk.

My sister remembers this as some sort of traumatic event in her adolescence but as far as I was concerned, that was the coolest thing I had seen by far. There are many such stories I remember from my childhood and I can't help but think that for all his faults, Dris made sure our lives never lacked for excitement.

After many years of being told by my siblings that I suffer from a mental disorder which involves falsifying past events, I sat down and gave Dris some serious thought. He had died a few months ago of cancer. He was in and out of hospital for a couple of years with a final three-month stint in hospital. All through those three months, my mother stayed with him in the hospital room every single day and night and refused to let anyone else take her place. She did this willingly and not out of any misplaced sense of duty.

While I know Dris loved my mom in his own twisted way, he did not exactly give her a good life. She struggled through life, both financially and emotionally, and had to give up on all her dreams along the way. Now, I would say that there is a good reason to drop the ball and run. But there was something about Dris that drew people to him. When he died, the number of people who reached out to say how he had touched their lives was astounding. He seemed to be able to do the right thing by everyone else other than his family.

I remember Dris with my niece. It was probably the only time that I have seen him expressing anything remotely resembling affection. He would carry her on his shoulders down to the store every day, with his back trouble and all. Strangely, it was not a very comforting thought that the man was capable of love. Makes me think that it was probably us, then. Or maybe he just came into his own as a grandfather. He wrote regular letters to my niece and later my son where he would cut out pictures from magazines and paste them in the letter with weird captions. An angry woman with a rolling pin: 'Angel face (that was what he called Amma in print) is in a bad mood today.' A man staring out of a window at the rain: 'Waiting for the seasons to change so that I can see you again.' You get the drift. Dris was quite a difficult man to read. Maybe he changed with time, maybe we all did. During the last years, we actually resembled a half-functional family. After Dris had been diagnosed with cancer Amma and he moved in with me. He was never dramatic about his situation and it didn't seem to bother him very much. That bothered me a lot for reasons I don't even begin to understand. I couldn't understand how he could possibly not be affected by the fact that he was dying. Throw in a lot of irrational

DRIS

guilt that these situations seem to conjure up and I almost started believing that he was the wronged one.

He went one day with minimum fuss and that was that. When I look back at his life, I can't help but think that he lived a full life. It is truly a blessing to want for so little and to think the absolute world of oneself. It is truly a recipe for happiness. So there you have the man. We may all have our opinions about him, but truth be told, he was by the far the most interesting of us all.

ANNA

Shashi Baliga

IT WAS THE day the fan was switched off.

One cruelly still afternoon, climbing up to the first floor of our one-storey house in search of a book, I found my father curled up in his bed, the fan switched off at the peak of a raging Madras summer. He had his back to me and he lay still; I couldn't make out if he was asleep or just switching off. I let him be.

That was the day it struck me that something was wrong.

'Anna, why didn't you put on the fan when you slept in the afternoon?' I asked him later in the evening.

'I couldn't bear the noise it made,' he replied off-handedly. From his point of view, it was a perfectly rational, unremarkable answer. I couldn't think of anything to say in argument or sympathy but I think I understood how fragile his emotional being had become.

He didn't mope in the popular sense of the term: wear a long face or a visibly troubled expression; cut himself off from the world. There were none of the standard giveaways. He just went about his work and life quietly and sat in a protective bubble of silence inside which you sensed a great turmoil. A man trying very hard to hold all the quivering pieces together.

ANNA

'Why is Doctor Ramdas so quiet today?' the occasional visitor or relative would remark, with a smile that was sometimes concerned, sometimes sly. 'Not in a good mood?'

He smiled, we smiled.

Because Doctor was not unnaturally quiet, just uncharacteristically so. Silence was not his natural state.

He was a man who could fill a room with his presence and laughter. At six feet and three inches, close to 200 pounds in his fifties and thereafter, he was a presence. He drew people to him easily. And he would then ply them with an unending supply of jokes and anecdotes drawn from his life and work.

We grew up hearing numerous tales (and variations thereof) from his medical college days, his cricketing years, the hospitals he ran, the petty bureaucracy of the Railways (where he worked), or our sprawling extended family. We heard about his tiffs and triumphs at work, about his nasty colleagues and his travels across India along familiar railway lines.

Dinner times and the family conversations that followed spilled over with stories, broadsides, raucous laughter and a continuous supply of food. (These were the days before television, when families actually sat down to talk after dinner.) We children were allowed to butt in whenever we wished to and encouraged to speak our mind at all times. He loved speech too much to curtail it, for himself or others. 'Speak up for what you believe in, or what you believe is the truth. And hang the consequences!' he would exhort us. (It's not, as I have discovered, a policy that always pays good dividends, but it does make life much simpler at one level.)

My mother, a widowed grand-aunt who lived with us, and the kitchen staff—collectively named the 'kitchen cabinet'—fed the troops untiringly. Meals served at the table were followed by the day's dessert in the living room. When my mother ran out of freshly-made sweets, she brought out the mithai. When she decided we'd had enough of those or wanted to conserve them for the next session, she switched to fried snacks. We did not think this eating pattern unusual; it was what we grew up on.

'Let's have some chaklis!' my father would declare after payasam. If he was reminded curtly by the kitchen cabinet that he had finished the chaklis the night before, he would roar with pride. And some other snack would be rolled out. Till, exhausted by the eating and the talking, he would finally ascend the stairs to his bedroom, trailed by a string of sleepy-eyed children.

Every day, he would be up early and insist, despite our plaintive and irritable complaints, on playing M.S. Subbulakshmi's Suprabbatham, the hymn sung to awaken his (and one presumes M.S. Subbulakshmi's) favourite god, Lord Venkateswara of Tirupati. It is a beautiful rendition but not one that young mortals deprived of precious early morning slumber can quite appreciate.

On school mornings, my mother would be busy downstairs in the kitchen, so it was my father who would herd us all into different bathrooms where our toothbrushes would be waiting for us in readiness, toothpaste squeezed out to the correct length. (He continued to do this for us till we got to our teens and finally rebelled.) All five children were packed off to school in a flurry of uniforms and shoes and shouted instructions. Peace would reign gratefully over the household till my father got back from office, we from school and homework, and the family caught up for dinner and a new round of anecdotes, food and family discussions.

Any time spent with my father was high-energy and usually

high-decibel. He liked to be surrounded by voices, words and noise (not always his own) at all times.

And there he was, that summer afternoon, sleeping with the fan switched off because he couldn't take the noise.

By then, we had got accustomed to seeing him in what we called 'his mood'. It was a catch-all word, this 'mood'. It could mean either of two extremes and a lot else in-between. It could mean he was the life of the house or the party, his voice booming over all conversation. Or that he was 'down' or 'low'—some more of the snap words we used.

They were the simplest words we had to describe the alternating spells of extroverted and introverted behaviour that we saw him go through. The gregariousness was, in isolation, no cause for alarm; it was but an exaggerated version of his familiar self. It was the downswing, his gradual slide into it and the slow climb out, that worried and puzzled us.

The Suprabbatham stopped playing in the mornings. We heard few stories at the dinner table. He ate well, but not extravagantly. And he went to bed early.

We couldn't understand.

But he did. He medicated himself; we saw him counting out his pills every morning and we were reassured that he was taking care of himself, just as he took care of all of us and the numerous medical problems that a large family of five children, their parents, grandparents and a grand-aunt was heir to.

Besides, we were armed with little information. The worldwide web had not yet circled the globe, information was not available in the privacy of your home. And this was not the sort of thing you talked about in the genteel middle-class enclaves of determinedly conservative Madras in the 1970s. It was a time when people did not speak of what were considered private matters; what went on inside a house stayed within it.

So, while we talked about those 'moods' and joked about them between ourselves, we didn't discuss them with anyone outside our immediate family. Or with him. It was the one subject that he didn't like to talk about—whichever end of the spectrum he inhabited at the time—and we sensed that he wanted to deal with it in his own way.

Besides, the lows didn't last too long and the highs were so entertaining. He was at his fulsome and generous best at the peaks; we got lots of hugs, kisses and unexpected gifts; guests and patients streamed into the house continuously and often unannounced; laughter filled the air. Friends, visitors and family were vastly entertained and patients queued up to see the doctor who always had a ready smile and a joke.

These were highly productive phases; even after he had retired from the Railways he kept himself (and us) busy the day through. So we rode the highs with him happily. They could be exhausting, but they were fun; it was like being on a prolonged family picnic.

The upside of the low side was that it was a breather. There was nothing abnormal about his behaviour, actually. If you had not seen him at his peak, you would merely think he was not given to much talk. At all times, he took his responsibilities as husband, father and provider enormously seriously and continued to do all that he saw as his duty. (The reprimand we heard most often was: 'Don't be so irresponsible!') Up or down, he was equally loving. It was the swings between the highs and lows that we had to adjust to.

I read up on this in the library. I learnt about what was called 'manic depressive disorder'. The word manic scared me at first, then I decided 'disorder' was the correct word for my father's behaviour. It was not normal for him, but it was not abnormal by general social parameters. It could exhaust us, irritate us sometimes (especially when it was a long story or a long silence), but I could say the same about dozens of other people then and now.

Everyone has eccentric aunts or uncles, teachers or colleagues who don't quite fit into accepted configurations of behaviour; that's what makes them interesting, if sometimes inconvenient. We didn't think of my father as eccentric, though; he just had his moods.

From here and there, in my other reading—books, newspapers, magazines, medical literature lying about at home—I also learnt that many great creative minds showed signs of this disorder and that made me feel better. Because my father was creative in his own way: he wrote long, funny, descriptive letters; he loved bad rhymes ('Every rose has its thorn and every loco its horn,' he would mock-intone on our many train travels when the engine driver leaned on the horn.)

He played on words, often moving from Konkani to English or Tamil or shaky, mispronounced Sanskrit, French or Italian, till we'd forget where he'd started off. Good work was never rewarded with 'Excellent!' but with 'Esculento!'; never mind that esculento did not mean excellent in Italian, but 'fit to be eaten' or 'edible'. Similarly, a disaster would always be labelled 'an horreur', pronounced 'hawroor' and with 'an' instead of 'une', despite my fervent objections. It was a tip of his hat to my becoming the first in the family to learn French, he said, and he would pronounce it his way. There were other verbal manoeuvres too complicated to explain here but what they did was teach us to play with language and words and to not let the rules restrain us—in this area at least.

He also bestowed bizarre nicknames on most people, including family. Once again, these nicknames straddled languages. One relative who was very particular about not wasting food and cleaning up his plate was, for instance, christened Khaali Prasad. The name came from a Railway workman my father had treated, but in this context the nickname was a play on the Konkani and Hindi 'khaali' which means empty. If we lingered too long over a meal, we would be ordered: 'Come on, be a Khaali Prasad!'

My father inherited his love of words and writing from my grandfather, who wrote a daily diary faithfully for decades, and my grandmother, who liked to cook up nonsense verse to amuse us kids. Thanks to all of them, we grew up with a free-spirited family vocabulary that meandered where and how it wished.

So, I decided, that's what it was: his moods were a manifestation of his creativity bubbling forth or brewing quietly inside, waiting for release. If his moods could be treated with medication, they were just a chemical reaction inside his body like, say, diabetes. He didn't have diabetes; he had this.

That was how it stayed for me till the end.

It was much, much later, as my reading and exposure grew with my journalistic career, that I added on bubbles of information about what was now being called bipolar disorder (sounds less scary, I guess). I picked up glimpses into the minds of people who had it or had family members who suffered varying degrees of it. A couple of my colleagues seemed to suffer from bouts of depression; I ventured some hesitant questions and to my half-surprise, they talked about it honestly. They were not pretty conversations.

ANNA

So that was what real depression, black and dangerous, was like, I thought to myself. Hearing about it from people who had gone through it and had the words to describe the subtlest or most painful mental shift was certainly very different from reading about it. One perfectly rebellious colleague told me of how he was 'simply too scared' to step outside his tiny apartment for days on end. Another, similarly felled, confided that she knew she was being illogical and foolish but couldn't do anything about it and it hurt because 'I know I'm smart'. She also knew she needed help but was, again, 'too scared' to go to a doctor (she eventually did, though).

And then there was Jerry Pinto. He wrote a lot for the paper I worked with at the time and we had all manner of conversations discussing story ideas, of which he never ran short. He was a smart, quick writer who never, ever let me down when it came to a deadline. But there were often caveats—he had to be home at specific times to look after his mother, so could we meet tomorrow? His mother was not well today; could I give him an extra day? I heard stray remarks about how he couldn't take up a full-time job because he never knew when he would be called home. I presumed his mother was an invalid and left it at that. I knew better than to probe into a parent's vulnerability.

But one day, after years of knowing him, I asked—why at that point, I do not know—what actually was wrong with her, what exactly she did when she was 'angry' that so terrified the family. I don't remember the context now, but I do remember exactly where he stood and I stood in a long corridor on the fourth floor of the Times of India building and the moment of revelation it was for me.

It was the first time I had talked to anyone about a loved one who was in a similar position (or so I had thought). It was, for me, a singularly frightening conversation, though Jerry was quite matter-of-fact—not dramatizing, not complaining—about his mother's problems. After that talk, my heart felt unfamiliarly heavy and I went back to my dark, airless cabin and my regulation office desk, its wood worn and scuffed, and sat very still for a long time. Was this what others had to go through? Days of panic and terror and heart-thumping worry? Of incomprehension and helplessness? Pain and little peace? How did they ever cope? Arrange their lives around the problem? Stay stable and loving and caring?

It struck me then, decades too late, how unfair we had all been to my father. How flimsy and selfish our complaints about his behaviour had been. How much worse he could have been but stopped himself from being. Or maybe it was luck that he didn't get worse.

Today, I ask myself: Would we have been kinder if we had had more information? Would that have made life easier—for him and for us? Should we have talked to a doctor—behind his back? There are no answers to my questions, of course. Perhaps it's better that way.

But other questions remain. What is normal? Is talking too much or laughing too little abnormal? Are there markers for the points at which behaviour slides from normal to quirky to strange to out of control to abnormal? When a parent or spouse or child or sibling or friend deviates from their norm, do we try to correct course for our sake or theirs? Who are we to judge the exact calibration of 'normal' for the world at large and those we are close to, in particular? Are we 'normal' ourselves? And the question that cuts closest to the bone for people like me: 'Am I going to get it, too?'

ANNA

Psychiatrists don't use the pairings of 'normal' and 'abnormal', 'sane' or 'insane', of course. But we are not psychiatrists and we do not live our emotional lives by medical doctrines. We make snap judgments in our heads where nobody can trip us up for political or psychiatric incorrectness.

Sometimes, we make these judgments about ourselves, too, and so much of that is linked to our personal histories. 'Am I going to get it, too?' is now embedded not too deep in my subconscious, pushed down by the accumulated weight of years of thinking about it.

But I use the words 'manic' and 'depressed' with the same casual disregard that the rest of my family does. We constantly accuse each other of being 'hyper', a word that's tossed around freely, especially by our children. Most of them have fond but brief and hazy memories of their grandfather, amplified by our stories about him. To them, creatures of the 21st, let-it-all-hang-out century, their Ajja was a fun guy. What seemed eccentric or erratic fifty years ago is perfectly acceptable or even desirable now. So much for normal.

The grandchildren love to hear of his exploits—stepping out in the brightly coloured lungi he had slept in to buy the first fish of the day ('So cool!'), taking cycle rickshaws instead of taxis ('People do that in Kolkata all the time; what's the big deal?'), buying plastic containers with a passion ('Why not, they're so cheap.'). He distributed his plastic purchases to anyone who'd take them—and we took a lot. I still use two containers and a soap dish that he gave me some thirty-five years ago, and my fondness for them is the subject of much family mirth. They've served me well all these years and I just might bequeath them to my daughter—and she just might use them in memory of her cool grandfather.

She and her cousins revel in hearing about Ajja's quirks and using the words and phrases he invented. Both traits seem to have flowered in his grandchildren whose conversations sometimes need annotations. Once strictly for family consumption, his linguistic creations now find their way into Gen Y's Facebook pages and their friends' vocabulary as well. Every once in a while, a question like this will pop up on the family group chat: 'Is 'pyoor' one of Ajja's words?' (Yes, it was. 'Pyoor' was how many South Indians pronounced 'pure', so how could it not enter his vocabulary?) My daughter once posted a cartoon on her Facebook page with a caption that said 'Insanity is all relative', and added one of her own: 'This cartoon was made for our phamily for sure.' (Phamily is her default spelling when she's with family or close friends.) The cartoon, by Edgar Argo, has a psychiatrist asking a woman on his couch: 'Do any of your relatives suffer from mental illness?' She replies with a bewildered wave of her hands: 'No…they all seem to enjoy it!!!'

I think Anna would have approved.

One of the two qualities he never lost was his sense of humour, even when the joke was on him.

The other was his moral compass. Call me maudlin but in my book that made him a better man than anyone else I have known.

'YOU DIDN'T KNOW HER WHEN SHE WAS NORMAL'

Parvana Boga Noorani

I MUST HAVE been fifteen or sixteen years old then. The long holidays had brought me to Ujjain. I was the oddity, a girl from the city, a girl in trousers. It was a place of multiple eyes and constant surveillance. I had not chosen to come to Ujjain; I was there because my parents had settled there. My father moved there when my mother had caused some disturbances with his business partner in Bombay.

The three Boga children did not move with them. My eldest sister, Nivedita, had been adopted by my mother's sister; she was given away when she was a little over two years old. The next sister had just been born then, and after a gap of three years, I was born. That summer in Ujjain, I was in between school and college, happy to spend time with my father, happy to get on to his motorbike and see the sights, happy to curl up with a book and read through long hot Central Indian afternoons. By this time, Nivedita was in Elphinstone College; my other sister in Calcutta.

I knew, we all knew, Mummy was 'not well'. When we were very young, we were told she was suffering from 'sunstroke', something that had happened to her in Delhi, where summers were terrifying.

PARVANA BOGA NOORANI

My dad, I think, went to Delhi and brought her back. I really don't remember much about this except feeling very left out as the adults tended to huddle together for discussions in hushed tones. Otherwise, it was just the way she was—she was mummy and we had to look after her. We had to bear with her. Once she even flooded the house, convinced it needed cleaning. It took us ages to get all the water out and the place dry enough to use. We knew she was not the standard-issue mother.

I remember her stomach being sensitive to the slightest bit of chilli; but one summer day she took a pound of grapes and put them in a bowl and announced that she was making wine. She stuck the bowl on a shelf and ignored it. The inevitable happened in the heat; a fungus grew over it and the whole thing fermented horribly. 'This,' she said, 'is wine,' and when we laughed, she sat down and ate it all. I remember watching her with horrified fascination; she was going to be ill, horribly ill. But she wolfed it down, fungus and all, and nothing happened. No, she was not the standard-issue mother.

One afternoon in Ujjain she seemed to want to prove it. I came home to find I had been locked out of the house. It was an old-fashioned house, full of connected rooms. Mummy didn't have to do much to keep me at bay.

'Do you want to come in?' she asked me.

'Of course I do.'

'Jump in over the balcony then,' she said.

It wasn't as if she was asking me to do anything athletic. The wall around the barsaati balcony was just a couple of feet high. I stepped across it, aware that everyone was watching me, the downstairs neighbours, the young men with unsettling eyes lounging in the street...

'YOU DIDN'T KNOW HER WHEN SHE WAS NORMAL'

Then she threw open the doors and shouted, 'Look, look, my daughter is completely mad! She's jumping over the walls even though the doors are open! She should be put in a mad house, poor thing.'

I went in and pushed her inside and slammed the door on those eyes and those neighbours.

'*You* are mad,' I shouted, ashamed and enraged. 'I'm not. You're the one who should be in a mad house, not me.'

For years I shouted those lines at her and then I realized there wasn't much point. My mother was not going to a mad house. My father was having none of that. Kobad Boga had wooed his Dolly with love letters and poems; he had won her reluctant heart and he was not giving up on her that easily.

'Beta,' he would say when I stormed at him about something she had done, 'You didn't know her when she was normal.'

I had some hints though. Dolly was born into a family of teachers. Her sister, Shirin Maneckshahna, had studied teaching under the legendary Madame Maria Montessori herself. Dolly was a mathematician; a gold medallist who would take nothing less than full marks in arithmetic from her children. She'd worked at Queen Mary's School and at the Delhi Public Library and the Tata Demographic Institute at Trombay. When I was four she had gone off to the US on an exchange programme for a year. She was selected to represent India—one of five people selected from different countries. She worked at the Minneapolis Public Library in Minneapolis, Minnesota for most of the time and then travelled all over Europe before she came back to Bombay. She was even interviewed by the *Milwaukee Journal* and told readers that children in India 'had a great thirst for reading'.

PARVANA BOGA NOORANI

While she was on her UNESCO-funded trip, my sister and I were looked after by my dad and Sunder (aka Sunni), our maid. I remember seeing Mummy off. She was going by ship and we went to the docks to see her off. When she came back a year later we went to the airport to receive her. I didn't recognize this person with short bobbed hair, in a black dress with huge flowers printed on it and high-heeled white shoes. Where was my mummy of the crisp cotton saris, hair neatly tied in a bun and an amazing bindi on her forehead? This was some strange-smelling woman who came back. Even her bags and clothes had that 'foreign' aroma for a long time, all of which have lingered in my olfactory memory. When she went to sleep, she put rollers in her hair and tucked everything into a nightcap, which made us laugh like mad.

She told us she had dolls for us in her luggage that was to follow. When that luggage did arrive, by steamer, we went to Ballard Estate and onto the ship to pick up the largest 'bag' I'd ever seen. It was a cabin trunk with wooden slats and brass rivets all over it. My sister got a walkie-talkie doll and I got one that drank water from a bottle and promptly peed. (I was determined to find out how this happened and swiftly proceeded to rip the head off the doll to check the insides. Needless to say that was the last time the doll peed.)

So who was my mother? The caring woman who taught several generations of women mathematics? Or was she the woman who cornered me one day when I came out of my bath, a wet and skinny ten-year-old, saying, 'Your sister's not here to protect you now, what are you going to do?'

I can't remember what it was about but I do remember my mouth going dry with fear and I remember yelling at her, 'You're crazy. Get out of here!' I remember running out of the bathroom

'YOU DIDN'T KNOW HER WHEN SHE WAS NORMAL'

and straight to the neighbour's house where I stayed until Sunni came to get me.

What do I tell you about her that will convey who she was? Do I tell you of the time I flippantly said to my dad, 'Why don't you divorce her?' He just looked at me and repeated that I hadn't known her when she was normal and I had to make allowances for her illness and understand. I also remember my dad teaching me to treat it as a joke and laugh—I guess just so that I wouldn't cry.

But what do you do, laugh or cry, when your mother is holding a knife at your neck and threatening to kill you when you're lying on the bed? It was a very sharp knife, its edge honed in the factory. I remember looking her in the eye and saying, calmly, very calmly, 'Now don't be stupid, just give me the knife.' Where did that calm come from? Looking back now, it must just have been the instinct to survive. If I had reacted abruptly, that knife might have slipped. The tension was incredible but I kept looking her in the eye, forcing her to maintain eye contact, forcing her to recognize me as the child she had named. Finally, she did give me the knife. I don't know if it was minutes or seconds; it seemed like hours. She made me promise I would go back to Bombay as soon as possible and not 'come between my husband and me'. I also remember my heart threatening to burst out of my body while trying to look and sound calm. Putting this down on paper right now my heart is hammering—and she's been dead over twenty years.

But again I also remember her when she was depressed. No amount of cajoling, yelling or coaxing could get her out of bed or get her to eat. At times like that she would lose weight and become half her size. She wouldn't talk, eat, bathe or read though ours was a house that was filled with books and we all read, all the time.

There were highs and there were lows and we knew how to deal with them...or at least learned how to deal with them—a lot of that learning was 'on the job' as it were. Over time we became adept at recognizing the different phases; all it would take was a twitch of the eye, a change in handwriting and we knew which stage was coming next. Somewhere inside of her she too knew. She always kept her meds handy and knew what to take when. Medication in those days was very primitive. When she was high they gave her downers and when she was depressed she was given uppers. When I look back upon this pill popping I guess she was a junkie on prescription meds, before it was fashionable to be so.

I also remember her when she was given electro-convulsive therapy, 'shock treatment' as it was called. She would come out of that Bellasis Road Nursing Home like a zombie, her words slurring, her eyes crazier than normal. Those were truly terrifying days.

Many years later, when I was flying with Air India, the doctors started prescribing Lithium Carbonate, which was virtually unavailable in India. I remember going into Boots in London and buying a bottle of 100 tabs for just one pound sterling! The Lithium was the only thing that kept her relatively stable, however it could not be given without a break as it affected the liver; so every six months or so she'd have to be taken off it. And we were back to square one.

I thank God for my aunts, her sisters; they were always there for us, surrogate mothers. Her older sister, Shirin, Mumsoo to us, had adopted my oldest sister, Nivedita, not legally but to all intents and purposes, when she was a baby. It only occurred to us much later in life that it was strange that Mummy gave away her first-born child. Mumsoo was principal of a boarding school in Khandala

'YOU DIDN'T KNOW HER WHEN SHE WAS NORMAL'

and we spent all our school holidays there. The boarding school had holidays during the monsoon and we (in Queen Mary's) had the normal May vacations. There my other sister and I revelled in books. We had the whole school library to pick from and my favourite place to read was in the fork of an old soapnut tree. The sturdy trunk branched out conveniently into three and formed the perfect nook to snuggle into and read all day long. I think I read all of Enid Blyton, Mallory Towers, Nancy Drew and most of P.G. Wodehouse sitting in that tree. Happy times, carefree times; so much so that we were loathe to return to Bombay. We dawdled all the way when we had to return. Sunni would take us in a bullock cart to the station and we'd jump off en route and give her a right run around before being caught, roundly smacked and put back onto the cart. Inevitably we would miss the train and return grinning to Mumsoo. Years later Mumsoo told us that she always sent us to the station a day earlier than we actually had to leave since we enjoyed the truancy so much!

My father had to make some difficult decisions. Nivedita was given to Mumsoo. My other sister was left in Bombay with Sunder, and Daddy when he was in town. I was sent off to boarding school in Khandala. I don't think my parents moved to Ujjain straight away but did so after a few years. Khandala was second home for me in any case, sometimes I feel it was my first home; so the transition wasn't too drastic. Yet, when I think back upon it I guess there was a certain sense of being abandoned and that has shaped a lot of my reactions today.

The one thing I've said all my adult life is that I can't blame any of my actions on my mother's illness. Yes, she was ill almost all the time I knew her. But that was when I was a child. As an adult I am responsible for my own actions. I feel it's a total cop-out to blame one's childhood for one's actions as an adult. And yet, sometimes I can't help but wonder whether I would have turned out differently if she were not manic-depressive. Today, at age sixty, there are a lot of questions but no one to turn to for answers. So I guess one just files it away in one part of the brain and carries on. Don't know what else to do!

Fire up the iPad, play games until the wrist, fingers, shoulder all go numb—that numbs the brain, too. You don't need to deal with the churning. Or you put it down on paper, hoping that the act of writing is the start of a healing process.

So many questions and not too many answers. Why did Daddy not send us off to one of his sisters? How could he not protect us from her madness? These were the questions my cousin, Dinaz Boga, suddenly brought up when I visited her in America in 2001. As part of this archaeological expedition into family history, I wrote to Dinaz recently and asked her what she could remember. Dinaz reminded me that my father was one of ten, the youngest in the lot. There were five brothers and five sisters, it was as if my paternal grandparents had planned it: first a girl, then a boy and so on and on until they got to Kobad and stopped. Perhaps that status as the baby of the family was what made it impossible for him to make any hard decisions. But he seems to have failed us often.

I wonder why we didn't fight harder to make Daddy find some other way for us to be a family. We were all made to believe that the needs of others had priority over one's own. I find that I hadn't even really thought about it until now. After all, you just grow up taking your reality for granted. As for Daddy, Dinaz put it well when she wrote to me that she often felt like hugging him with one arm and shaking him with the other until his teeth rattled.

'YOU DIDN'T KNOW HER WHEN SHE WAS NORMAL'

And yet, I don't really think I was unhappy. The aunts, God bless their souls, provided oceans of love, care and nurture. Daddy, on the other hand, seemed to live more and more in a world of his own. Somewhere along the line, while I was with Air India, he suffered a heart attack and mummy then went to live with her sisters.

At one point, I don't remember exactly when, Mummy suffered from a detachment of the retina and she went off to a doctor and had surgery for it. Subsequently she lost her vision in both eyes. For years she was almost totally blind. Then some years later, Jaslok Hospital had some German doctors who were visiting and conducting eye surgery with some new method, both for cataracts and other eye problems. We took her there and she was operated upon following which she got back around ten per cent of her vision. After that she came and stayed with Muna, my husband, and me during her recovery period.

The last decade, or more, of her life was spent with her sisters Amy and Shirin. About a month before Mummy died, Amy called Nivedita and me and asked us to come to Navsari where she'd been looking after Mummy. She said she was exhausted and couldn't do it anymore. We went to Navsari. The first shock was Amy; she seemed to have aged ten years. But nothing prepared us for the sight of the creature my mother had become. She spent the entire night screaming that someone had stolen her 'chaddis' (panties) and her money. She wouldn't keep any clothes on and was constantly soiling herself. Amy had finally just put a mattress on the floor with a plastic sheet on it. Mummy couldn't be left alone on a bed as she had fallen off a few months earlier and broken her hip. She did not recognize either Nivedita or me.

Amy wanted us to take a decision. We called a local psychiatrist who told us that our mother was probably schizophrenic and not bipolar. At that point we couldn't have cared less what label he put on her. All we wanted was for her to be given some medication that would ease her nightmares. He suggested we commit her to an asylum. Shirin, aka Mumsoo, simply refused. She said that as long as she was alive her sister would not go to an asylum. At that point Mumsoo, who was well into her seventies, took up a job as administrator of an orphanage in Surat. The only stipulation she made was that they allow her a room for her sister in the adjoining old people's home.

The rest of us returned to our lives; we knew that the sorority had taken over. Dolly was safe; Mumsoo was handling her; Amy could rest.

One month later, it was all over.

Weeping into the mayonnaise that was to cover the 'whole cold poached salmon' that I was making for a catering contract I had committed to that day, I managed somehow to get all the food to the client before Nivedita, Daddy, my cousin Dinoo Dalal and I climbed into two Ambassador cars that Muna had rented and started on our journey to Surat late at night. When we got there in the morning, we went straight to the Towers of Silence and for the first time, in my memory, I saw my mother totally at peace. The face was serene. No frown lines, no worry marks, no tortured looks.

Just serenity.

At last.

SOME QUESTIONS FOR A BROTHER

Ina Puri

HE LOOKED DISTINCTLY out of place in that Emergency Ward, smartly dressed as always in shades of beige and brown, in only the finest—from his suit and tie to his polished-to-a-shine shoes. Only that thing around his neck did not belong to my brother; a ghastly green plastic rope, sawed off shabbily at the ends when they brought him down. That and his face, eyes bulging, tongue out and mottled. I did not know how to respond. How does one respond to something like that?

Instead, I went about dusting his suit and rearranging his arm, which was dangling at an odd angle from the stretcher. The doctors declared him 'dead on arrival'.

I could deal with an arm dropped off a stretcher. But when they returned him from the mortuary, they had wrapped him up in sheets and tied him up with ropes.

Did Arijit Lahiri, beloved brother, think of what was to come when he made his decision? Did he know his clothes would be torn off him and his insides poked at by strangers? Did he think about it as he went about organizing the day? When the body is finally consumed by fire, all that you have left are questions.

We rehearsed his last day incessantly, picking over it for clues. We heard he walked the dogs, whom he adored, then gulped down his breakfast and drove off, cheerfully fixing to meet his wife and her parents for lunch. From colleagues' accounts, we heard it had been another hard day at the office. He had his usual simple lunch of daal and sabzi and then drove out. After office, he had made a detour to the market. He stopped to buy the plastic rope he needed and then went on to hang himself from the ceiling fan in the old house they had lived in before they moved to a more fashionable gated community. His laptop and briefcase were placed neatly on a chair. His wife found him that evening in their erstwhile home.

In retrospect, I was relieved when we took him home that last time, I in the front of the van, him, draped in sheets, at the back. The driver played the radio and I began to accept that it was all over. We were alone then, he and I, not laughing about some silly joke or quarrelling even, just silent. My questions to him began in that moment and I have never stopped asking. Okay, we'd had it tough, he and I. But Arijit, you're supposed to fight, right? You're not supposed to cop out, right? He didn't answer. Maybe dead people laugh and the living can't hear them. I would like to believe that he was laughing, showing his tormentors the finger as we trundled over the potholes and made our way home. His home. The keening of the dogs brought the first rush of tears to my eyes. Kit Kat and Nutty knew immediately what had taken me twenty-four hours to realize. He was gone.

That year he hadn't come home for raakhi (*Should I have guessed?*), and the last time we spoke he had said we would meet and talk about things that were not going so well in his life. (*Should I have insisted he come over immediately?*) Over the years, we had

SOME QUESTIONS FOR A BROTHER

grown apart, busy with our own lives and work (*Should I not have found time for him?*), but he called, usually on his way to office. I invariably told him to drive carefully; he would laugh and continue chatting: about Ma, or Arjun, my son and his favourite nephew, or his dogs and mine. I'll always think of him like that: a whiff of expensive aftershave, Ray-Ban glares and blaring music as he drives off, hand raised in a quasi-salute.

With that image comes a memory. Our parents had gone to Europe and we had the run of the flat for a fortnight. I was at home, reading, when a very harried and hassled Arijit came rushing in, completely out of breath. He was learning how to ride a motorbike and he had rammed it straight into a police van! Flustered and nervous, he had invited the cops to our flat with the offer of tea and omelettes if they let him off. The police did let him off with a reprimand but he never practised riding the motorbike in the neighbourhood again…

This boy grew up, and before he was fifty he killed himself. No note. No accusations. No remonstrations.

The ringtone on his phone played his favourite Hindi film song from *Dil Apna aur Preet Parai*: 'Ajeeb daastaan hai yeh, kahaan shuroo, kahaan khatam…' I re-examined the lyrics of the song, wondering if there was a hint there that I had missed. 'This is a strange tale, where does it begin, where does it end…'

In the clarity of my head I know I am not to blame. In the dark recesses of my heart, guilt seems to have found a home.

As a young boy he loved the cinema and when Baba took him to see *Battle of the Bulge*, he was sleepless with excitement. We lived in a modest flat in Union Park, Bandra, Bombay and the imagined roar of battle filled the rooms for days. Our games were mostly play-acting and improvising, because we did not have too many toys. So a ruler would double up as a gun and a dining chair as a war tank. Then, he saw *Bramhachari* with a visiting uncle and lost his heart to the Good Samaritan Shammi Kapoor for a long while. He tried to hide his tears when he narrated the story to our help, Gyanada, whom he adored. I teased him and that made him very angry. Ma and Baba took his side, and that made me angry.

My parents adored their son and I often felt ignored in those early years. Left out of their games and treats. I have often thought that it was the divorce our parents went through that left him off-centre. He couldn't cope with the absence of our father and showed his resentment in many small, odd ways. It was even more awkward when my mother remarried and found happiness with our stepfather. We reacted in our own ways. I was delighted to meet Bapi and happily learned to consult him on every little matter. My brother was wary, diffident. Things got better when our little brother Shamya was born because we both loved him unequivocally. Arijit accused me of loving the new entrant a little more than I loved him, and that was partly true. As the older sister my attention and love transferred to this curly-haired baby who became the centre of my universe. If Arijit felt betrayed, I was guilty.

My brother ended up playing serious cricket for the State Under-19 Team and was a good student at St Xavier's College. Shamya hero-worshipped him and for a long period of time went to school with the Under-19 Cricket Team's cap hidden in his school bag to show off to his classmates. Then I got married and moved away from home, to live in another city.

What causes depression? Many tiny moments of sadness or one traumatic legacy that sweeps you in a storm that you never recover from? And what is the tipping point? When does the

SOME QUESTIONS FOR A BROTHER

burden become so great that it makes someone who is depressed take his own life?

For months afterwards, friends and family who had seen him grow up were shocked that Arijit could take his own life. In the family, he was known, after all, for his dry, deadpan sense of humour that spared no one. When he held forth, we cracked up.

Was he trying to lighten Ma's mood that last time he called hours before he died? All she could say, disbelievingly, when she heard the news was that he seemed to be in such a jovial mood that morning, teasing her and joking about relocating to Kolkata and finding a new job, any job that would be less pressure, even if it meant opening a kirana dukan (a grocery store) in Jodhpur Park where she lived.

We looked for answers. The doctors said he was 'clinically depressed' and that this was probably caused by the brain haemorrhage he had suffered some years earlier. Others said it was office politics that left him feeling defeated. Yet others spoke of the difficult situation at home. But there didn't seem to be much more than any man in his late forties faces. And even as I think this, there is a fresh feeling of guilt. Who am I to judge what a man can bear and what he cannot?

Just a few months earlier, when my son was visiting from London, Arijit had taken him out for a spin and made plans to see him soon. 'Just us,' he had said, winking conspiratorially. 'We'll have a blast!'

Seven years have passed, but closure still evades us. We repeat those questions in our heads and still search for some sliver of an answer. In vain.

On the 7th of March every year we remember him and, fittingly, there is complete irreverence in the homage we pay him. I think of the man who often said, 'I am too old for Rock 'n' Roll and too young to die.'

Was that a clue?

Two night-time stories come back sometimes as shadows gather and regrets return. The first is being woken up from a dead sleep, a sleep of emotional exhaustion brought on by the intense and solemn memorial service for my stepfather on his first death anniversary. Shamya's wife Ajitha is shaking my arm.

'What is it?' I ask.

'I don't want to frighten you but Dada has set the bed on fire.'

Of course, he's a bit overwrought, I think. But he shouldn't have been smoking in bed. He shouldn't have been smoking in the first place.

'Do you want to kill yourself?' I ask.

He pauses for a second, with a comic's timing, and then guessing perhaps that it is not the time for a smart answer, says, 'No.'

What would his real answer have been?

The second: It is night, a cold night. We are all snuggled down and enjoying the warmth of our blankets, enjoying that rare thing: a winter night in Bombay. I must have been ten and Arijit six. Outside we hear a beggar calling for alms, bemoaning his fate, the cold night. I am about to duck my head under the pillow and cut him out when Arijit gets up and rushes to the window, bearing his blanket aloft. He throws open the window and calls to the beggar. 'Dada, yeh lena,' he shouts and the blanket flies out into the night, a harbinger of hope.

I wonder sometimes whether all Arijit needed was someone to open a window somewhere and throw him a blanket.

Was that someone supposed to be me?

Sleep well, little brother.

NOTES ON THE CONTRIBUTORS

Shashi Baliga is an independent journalist, media educator and Executive Director, Literature Live!, organizers of Tata Literature Live!, Mumbai's annual literary festival. She lives with her husband in Mumbai; their daughter and her husband are based in Dubai. Her family is scattered across the world—her mother and elder sister live in Chennai, her younger sisters in Kolkata and Baltimore, her brother in Toronto. The extended family's list of nicknames and family jokes is ever on the increase, with four generations adding to it avidly.

Leela Chakravorty is a pseudonym for a mechanical engineer in the corporate sector whose personal interest lies in pursuing literature and teaching.

Sukant Deepak is an associate editor with the India Today Group and writes on art and artists. Associated with different newspapers and magazines as a freelancer and staffer from the age of sixteen, he has always wanted to write fiction but the blank computer screen scares him no end. He lives alone in Ambala and is a self-confessed recluse. Passionate about reading, motorcycling and travelling, he hopes to do some translations and write his book when the blank screen stops terrifying him.

Nirupama Dutt is Chandigarh's own home-grown poet, journalist, art and literary critic and translator. She writes in both English and Punjabi as well as occasionally in Hindi. She is the author of *The Ballad of Bant Singh*, the biography of a Dalit activist and singer of Punjab. Her other books include her poetry collections *Ik Nadi Sanwali Jahi* (winner of

NOTES ON THE CONTRIBUTORS

the Punjabi Akademi Award) and *The Black Woman*; *Stories of the Soil* (a collection of landmark stories from Punjabi, in English translation) and *Poet of the Revolution* (a translation of the memoirs and poetry of Lal Singh Dil). She has also translated a collection of poems by Gulzar, *Pluto*, into English. Nirupama is currently working on her first novel.

Annabelle Furtado (a pseudonym) writes for a number of publications located in the Middle East from the comfort of her home. In the past she worked full time at media outlets in Mumbai and Bangalore. She spends most of her time raising her children, nurturing an organic garden and writing short stories that she hopes will one day be published. She is based in Bangalore.

Lalita Iyer is a Bombay-based journalist and writes on relationships, food, parenting and travel. Her work has appeared in *Man's World*, the *Hindustan Times*, the *Times of India*, *The Indian Express*, *Vogue*, *Elle* and *National Geographic Traveller*. She is the author of *I'm Pregnant, Not Terminally Ill, You Idiot!* and *The Boy Who Swallowed a Nail and Other Stories*.

Sharmila Joshi is a pro-bono editor at the People's Archive of Rural India (PARI), an online multi-media archive, and a consulting editor at Gateway House: Indian Council on Global Relations, a foreign policy think tank. She is also an occasional writer, researcher and teacher. She has previously worked as a full-time or freelance journalist at various publications. Her academic background is in historical sociology, and her areas of interest include globalization, gender and inequality. Sharmila lives in Mumbai, but decades after moving still sometimes misses a long-gone lane and forever-lost home in Nagpur.

Manoj Menon studied law at the National Law School, Bangalore, worked in Mumbai with an accounting firm, a law firm and a dot com company, and has now settled down in Bangalore with his wife and three children.

Patricia Mukhim is currently Editor, *The Shillong Times*, Meghalaya's largest circulating English daily which was started in 1945. She has been a

NOTES ON THE CONTRIBUTORS

high school teacher for two decades and a single mother to four children, three daughters and a son. Her second daughter passed away in 2008, seven months after her marriage. Patricia writes regular columns for the *Statesman*, *The Telegraph* and the *Assam Tribune*. She tries to use journalism as an advocacy tool for women's issues and mental health causes.

Parvana Boga Noorani has worn many hats in her life: daughter, sister, niece, lover, wife, aunt, airhostess, banker, caterer, food writer, friend. But the one she cherishes most is friend.

Ina Puri is a writer, biographer, art curator and collector. She is the author of several books, including *In Black & White* (a biography of the artist Manjit Bawa), *Faces of Indian Art* (iconic artists seen through the lens of Nemai Ghosh) and *Journey with a Hundred Strings* (on the music and life of Pandit Shiv Kumar Sharma). She produced *Meeting Manjit*, a film on Bawa, her friend and collaborator, which won a National Award. She is Editor at *Art Varta* and has recently published a pictorial memoir on Pt. Shiv Kumar Sharma entitled *The Man and His Music*. She has also edited Raghu Rai's *Kolkata*, the distinguished photographer's visual narrative of the city and its people. Ina's three-decade-long engagement with the arts embraces everything from tribal art and folk theatre to contemporary performing arts, visual arts and literature. She lives in Gurgaon with her husband Ravi, son Arjun, and canine soulmate Leyla.

Amandeep Sandhu is a writer who remains bewildered at how mental health is at the centre of so many crises in the world but gets such little attention. He is the author of two partly autobiographical novels: *Sepia Leaves*, a story of a boy growing up in the shadow of schizophrenia, and *Roll of Honour*, about the split loyalties of a Sikh adolescent in the year 1984. *Roll of Honour* was nominated for The Hindu Literary Prize 2013. He is now working on a non-fiction book on Punjab. In 2013-15 he was a Fellow at Akademie Schloss Solitude, Stuttgart. Much before that he earned his bread through journalism and teaching. Later he earned butter and honey as a technical writer in the IT industry. Currently he is jobless.

NOTES ON THE CONTRIBUTORS

Madhusudan Srinivas is in his mid-fifties, a resident of Delhi, and mostly a resident of Planet Autism, along with his son Abhimanyu, who is in his early twenties. In their professional avatar, Madhu and his significant other are journalists, hacks left over from the print-dominated era of the 1980s. Madhu now holds a day job as senior news editor with NDTV, which he believes is India's premier and most credible news channel (:-)). But mind and heart, 24/7, live on Planet Autism, where a residency was obtained in 1995, when Abhimanyu was diagnosed. For the record, father and son swim, roller skate, and walk and walk and walk. And drive and drive and drive, and listen to music of all sorts. After all that there's life too, friends to be met, and parties to be gone to.

Jerry Pinto is the author of *Em and the Big Hoom* (winner of the Windham-Campbell Prize, the Hindu Literary Prize and the Crossword Book Award for Fiction) and *Helen: The Life and Times of an H-Bomb* (winner of the National Award for the Best Book on Cinema). His other works include *Asylum*, a book of poems; and translations (from Marathi) of Daya Pawar's autobiography *Baluta*, Sachin Kundalkar's novel *Cobalt Blue* and Vandana Mishra's memoir *I, the Salt Doll*. He has also edited several anthologies, including *Bombay, Meri Jaan: Writings on Mumbai* (with Naresh Fernandes).

www.ingramcontent.com/pod-product-compliance
Lightning Source LLC
Chambersburg PA
CBHW052051220426
43663CB00012B/2532